STUDIES IN HISTORY, ECONOMICS, AND PUBLIC LAW

EDITED BY THE FACULTY OF POLITICAL SCIENCE
OF COLUMBIA UNIVERSITY

Number 299

JAPAN'S FOREIGN EXCHANGE AND HER BALANCE OF INTERNATIONAL PAYMENTS

WITH SPECIAL REFERENCE TO

Recent Theories of Foreign Exchange

JAPAN'S FOREIGN EXCHANGE AND HER BALANCE OF INTERNATIONAL PAYMENTS

WITH SPECIAL REFERENCE TO

Recent Theories of Foreign Exchange

BY

S. Y. FURUYA

AMS PRESS
NEW YORK

COLUMBIA UNIVERSITY
STUDIES IN THE
SOCIAL SCIENCES

299

The Series was formerly known as
Studies in History, Economics and Public Law

Reprinted with the permission of Columbia University Press
From the edition of 1928, New York
First AMS EDITION published 1968
Manufactured in the United States of America

Library of Congress Catalogue Card Number: 68-58576

AMS PRESS, INC.
NEW YORK, N.Y. 10003

PREFACE

DURING and after the World War, exchange was one of the popular topics of discussion which demanded clear thinking. Practically all nations except the United States suffered from dislocated exchanges. Yet the theories as to the causes and remedies of these abnormal exchanges differed a great deal among the writers of different countries. Cassel, Keynes and most of the English economists have supported some form of the purchasing-power-parity theory, while other European economists adhered to a "speculation" theory, a "budgetary" theory, or a "reparation" theory. American economists were also divided in their opinions. But not all were satisfied with the line of thought developed by Viscount Goschen, Ricardo and J. S. Mill, for the classical theory of foreign exchange did not throw sufficient light upon the explanation of recent exchange movements. To say that exchanges are determined at the juncture of supply and demand is easy. But the matter is not quite so simple. We want to go a step farther, and ascertain what are the real conditions that determine supply and demand.

Various surveys of actual foreign exchange history have been recently made in different countries, but very few agree as to results. Taking this opportunity, the writer presents in the following study the Japanese case. Not belonging to any school or camp in the present exchange controversies, the author has tried to present the case as fairly as possible. Unfortunately, however, he has reached the conclusion that none of the recent exchange theories is adequate to explain the Japanese experiences.

His next step was to examine theoretically these various controversial theories. Then an attempt was made to reach a final form of exchange theory; and the author believes that if European economic situations were explained in terms of this theory, the nature of the recent dislocation of exchanges would have been better conceived and more clearly understood, without the internal contradictions and defects common to recent theories.

In order to explain the exchange situation in Japan, the writer has endeavored to present all the factors and movements which make up Japan's balance of international payments, especially during the period 1914-1927. The statistical presentation of this part of the study is original, although the author is aware of the fact that figures of this kind need further correction and refinement. The first chapter was written primarily for those who are not familiar with the economic organization of Japan.

The author must express his gratitude to both Professor H. Parker Willis and Professor James W. Angell of Columbia University, without whose kind assistance and suggestions this study might not have been written. He is also under obligation in a number of ways to Professors Seligman, Seager, Moore, Simkhovitch, Mitchell, Clark and others of Columbia University, to the managers of the Yokohama Specie Bank and the Bank of Japan, and to officials of the Financial Division of the Department of Finance and of the Commercial Division of the Department of Commerce and Industry of the Japanese government.

S. Y. Furuya.

New York City, August 15, 1927.

CONTENTS

LIST OF TABLES

LIST OF CHARTS

CHAPTER I

Introduction

1. THE OBJECT OF THIS SURVEY

THE Japanese yen as a problem of foreign exchange is worth studying from two angles: first, in practice; second, in theory. From a practical view, it has been the problem of Japan how to stabilize her widely fluctuating exchanges so that her foreign trade, bonds and credits may be least impaired. This was especially the case when her exchange rates fell more than 24 per cent below par without a corresponding increase of inflation during 1924. The trade of Japan, as well as her industries—especially her cotton and silk textile industries and sericulture—were seriously hurt by the exchange fluctuations, as the prosperity of these industries and trade has been much dependent upon and interrelated with the stabilization of the Japanese foreign exchange.

Whether Japan can return to the gold basis is another question. Both borrowers in Japan and lenders abroad are equally interested in her return to the gold basis. For, again, Japanese foreign bonds are greatly dependent upon and interrelated with the international value of the yen which is generally taken as the barometer of the country's prosperity and credit. But how can Japan return to the gold basis, and when?

There is still a third practical question; namely, the continuance, or displacement in favor of some other system, or absolute stoppage, of the long-continued system of a gold exchange fund. Is it advisable for Japan to continue this system or to change it? But again, the advisability or inadvisability of such a step is closely inter-related with the nature of the Japanese yen exchange and its characteristic fluctuations.

Unless, therefore, the Japanese yen exchange is well studied and scientifically scrutinized, any suggestion or proposal for the solution of these practical problems is impossible.[1]

But apart from these practical questions, there is a theoretical side. Why was the Japanese yen strong during 1914-1919? Why did it become weak after 1919? And how? What were the real causes of the great slumps of 1924 and 1925? Why is it recovering now? Under what principle or theory of foreign exchange can all this be explained? Or, to put it in a more precise form, what principle or theory of foreign exchange can inductively be arrived at from all the exchange movements of the Japanese yen?

[1] No such attempt has yet been made. In Japanese there have appeared a few books, such as K. Maeda's, *A Study of Japanese Yen Exchange*, Tokio, 1925, and J. Inoue's, *Japan's Financial and Economic Situations after the War*, Tokio, 1925, and also *Japan's International Finance at Present and her Policy*, Tokio, 1926, and the present writer's *Foreign Exchange*, revised edition, 1925. But all these are inadequate either in materials embodied or method pursued and length of period covered. In English or in other European languages, no treatise on the Japanese Yen or Yen Exchange has yet appeared, as far as the author knows. Such writers as Mr. Spalding and Dr. Mahlberg have touched the Japanese exchange very inadequately, giving only few pages, describing not more than what a casual traveler can report; besides their descriptions are rather out of date in spite of the fact that they were written recently. *Vide*, William F. Spalding, *Eastern Exchange, Currency and Finance* (London, 1917), 4th ed., London, 1924, pp. 126-170. Walter Mahlberg, *Uber asiatische Weckselkurse*, Leipzig, 1920, pp. 69-71. Even the United States Senate Commission of Gold and Silver Inquiry has omitted the Oriental exchanges entirely.

Will the classical theory of foreign exchange hold good? Or will the newer type of balance-of-payments theory meet this particular Japanese situation? Or more recently, much is spoken of the purchasing-power-parity theory. But can it explain adequately the Japanese yen fluctuations? More lately we hear of the speculation theory.[1] But is this the correct theory of foreign exchange?

A survey like this may at first seem to cover too narrow and too limited a field. But inasmuch as the study of foreign exchange is the study of the value of some one country's money in terms of foreign currencies, a survey of yen exchange cannot but bring out all those factors and elements which are connected or correlated in determining the value of the yen. But to do so requires not merely an exposition of the Japanese economic situation but also necessitates some study of economic situations in all other related countries. So our second thought will bring forth, after all, that the study of the Japanese yen exchange is by no means a narrow field, but on the contrary is one of the widest and most complicated of economic subjects.

Furthermore, Westerners must not be satisfied with the analysis of their foreign exchange situations and make hasty conclusions as to *the* theory of foreign exchange. A survey like this, from a purely theoretical standpoint, if not from that of practical importance, may rightly justify its existence. For, though not directly concerned, it is yet sufficient to test the strength of various foreign exchange theories and to help to arrive at a fuller and more significant theory of

[1] For the sake of brevity I so name it. For particulars, see my later discussion. Here it is sufficient to mention such writers as Prof. J. H. Williams, "German Foreign Trade and the Reparations Payments," *Q. J. of Econ.*, 1922, pp. 502-3; Prof. A. A. Young, "War Debts, External and Internal," *Foreign Affairs*, 1924, pp. 402-5; Prof. James W. Angell, *The Theory of International Prices*, Cambridge, 1925, pp. 426-27; de Bordes, *The Austrian Crown, London*, 1924, pp. 172-176.

foreign exchanges. To such an end, then, this survey is set forth.

The central thought running through this survey, however, is not only to scrutinize and to present a true picture of the external value of the yen, but to contend that none of the existing exchange theories can remain true, and that either they should be completely modified or a new theory should be formulated so that any exchange phenomenon may best be explained in the light of that theory.

2. GENERAL ECONOMIC BACKGROUND

Japan proper is not as large as California, but her coast line extends over 27 thousand kilometers. This narrow strip of islands lying in the temperate zone of the North Pacific contains 60 million people, or 157 persons per square kilometer, with a tendency to increase at the rate of 800 thousand people per year.[1] Does the land support the people? Or can the people find enough foods and comforts? Let us see how they are getting along.

In the first place, agriculture is waning. Roughly two-thirds of the territory is mountainous, only one-sixth of the land is arable. There are but 2,920,000 hectares of rice fields with scarcely any hope to increase either acreage or productivity beyond the present stage. On the other hand, the population is pressing upon the land. The result is over-intensive cultivation, exhaustion of soil, expensive farming with scant reward, tenancy disputes and, finally, village desolation. But as rice is the chief diet for the Japanese and in order to quiet the urban population, the government usually puts no import duties on rice, seeking to keep the price down. So we have to import every year 18 to 120 million yen worth of rice from China, Siam, French Indo-China and British India.

[1] An average of the last 5 years.

Sericulture is somewhat better, but not much. The difference is between hunger and bare subsistence. Were it not for sericulture, Japanese villages would have been ruined long ago.[1] The obstacles to sericulture are: (1) rent of upland is too high, (2) wages are too high, (3) price of cocoons is unstable. Rent of upland is high because land is scarce in Japan. Wages are relatively high because industrial districts are withdrawing farm hands with higher wages. The price of cocoons is unstable because cocoons are perishable goods like fruits or vegetables, and the ordinary peasant-farmer has no means to dry them. Furthermore, there is no product in Japan whose price is more fluctuating than that of raw silk. Of course, there are other reasons, but these are some of the outstanding facts why the Japanese peasant-farmer is not well paid.

Nor is Japan favored with minerals. Coal is not enough to meet the domestic consumption unless Manchurian coal is imported. Iron must also be imported to the amount of 200 million yen annually. So also petroleum; the home production of oil is only one-half of what is needed, or 15 to 25 million yen of oil must be imported. Before the War, Japan was second to the United States as a copper-exporting country. But since the War, she has had to import more than she exports.[2]

On the other hand, Japan has Chosen (Korea), Taiwan (Formosa), Bokoto (Pescadores) and Karafuto (Japanese

[1] The annual production of cocoons is 6 to 7 million *koku*, amounting in value 600 to 700 million yen. (1 *koku* = 5.11902 bushels) (1 yen = c49.85.)

[2] The production of other minerals are as follows: (year, 1926)

	Quantity (million)	*Value* (million yen)
Gold	8 grammes	13
Silver	126 "	6
Copper	66 Kg	53
Lead	6 "	1

Sagaline), the total area of which is nearly equal to that of Japan proper. The total population of these territories is, however, 22 million according to the census of 1925. In addition to these, Japan controls Kwantung Province by right of lease. All these territories produce raw materials which Japan needs. As for markets, China with 400 million people, India with 300 million people, the South Seas and Asiatic Russia are near Japan both geographically and commercially.

Under such circumstances it is but natural that she should be transformed into an industrial-manufacturing country. Whereas from 1912 to 1923 the area of rice fields increased only by 4% and the total output of rice by 10% (without considering increase of population), the paid-up capital of all industries in Japan increased from 870 million dollars to 5,100 million dollars (without considering decrease in the value of money) or almost six times in 11 years. In 1912 the total bills cleared were 4,800 million dollars. But in 1923 these increased to 34,000 million dollars or almost seven times. Fifty years ago we had no railroads, no steamships and no cities; but to-day we have 10,000 miles of railroads, 3,000,000 gross tons of steamships and hundreds of growing cities which already contain 12 million people, or one-fifth of the entire population. Thirty years ago we had only 2,910 factories run by motive power and 437,000 factory workers, but to-day we have 37,000 factories and 1,789,000 workers, an increase of twelve times in the former and four times in the latter case. To show details of this growth, the following table may be presented.

One of the salient features of the development of Japan's industry is the plentiful supply of hydroelectric power. In 1907 there were in all 69,000 kilowatts generated; but in 1923 this supply was increased to 3,058,000 kilowatts.[1] To-

[1] Department of Finance, *Kinyu Jiko Sankosho*, Tokio, 1924, pp. 196-7.

GROWTH OF FACTORIES IN JAPAN [1]

	Number of Factories			*Factory Workers*		
	With motive power	*Without motive power*	*Total*	*Male*	*Female*	*Total*
1897	2,910	4,377	7,287	182,000	254,000	437,000
1907	5,207	5,731	10,938	257,000	385,000	643,000
1917	14,310	6,656	20,966	567,000	713,000	1,280,000
1926	37,141	11,253	48,394	859,000	929,000	1,789,000

day one is surprised to see that even a very remote village is supplied with electric light, and the man-power is gradually being replaced by motor-power. Here and there one will see hydraulic power plants being built and high-voltage wires stretched all over the country.

Wages are relatively high in Japan not merely because the index numbers of money wages since 1922 are higher than the index numbers of general prices but more fundamentally because laborers are less efficient than in the Western countries.[2] They work more emotionally than rationally, and more traditionally than scientifically. Consequently, they waste much time and energy. However, inefficient are not only workers but also the whole industrial system of the country. For the sake of comparison, the following wage scales may be contrasted.

[1] In this table, government factories and workers are not included. There are at present about 380 government factories and 180,000 workers. Besides these numbers, there are about 350,000 mining workers and about 2,000,000 other miscellaneous non-factory workers.

[2] *Cf.* S. Uyehara, *The Industry and Trade of Japan*, London, 1926, pp. 326-7. For theoretical ground, see F. W. Taussig, *International Trade*, New York, 1927, pp. 35-6, 174-7.

AVERAGE DAILY WAGES OF LABORERS[1]

(1 yen = 49.85 cents)

	1920	1921	1922	1923	1924	1925
Textile Industry	*yen*	*yen*	*yen*	*yen*	*yen*	*yen*
Silk-reeler (female)	.98	.93	1.02	.93	.96	.97
Cotton-spinner (female)	1.10	1.04	1.11	1.07	1.10	1.16
Silk-thrower (female)	.88	.88	.90	.90	.91	.88
Cotton-weaver (male and female)	.85	.97	.99	.95	.94	.97
Silk-weaver (male)	1.19	1.30	1.12	1.05	1.16	1.13
Hosiery-knitter (male)	1.51	1.59	1.78	1.71	1.75	1.72
Hosiery-knitter (female)	.82	.81	.86	.87	.92	.89
Index numbers for above	97.0	99.1	102.1	99.1	102.0	101.6
Index numbers of prices	131.2	101.4	98.5	104.3	104.3	102.4
Manufacturing of Metal and Machine						
Lath-man	2.21	2.22	2.39	2.33	2.31	2.33
Finisher	2.19	2.22	2.35	2.38	2.33	2.38
Founder	2.23	2.14	2.27	1.98	2.21	2.25
Blacksmith	2.24	2.13	2.15	2.13	2.18	2.24
Wooden pattern maker	2.52	2.30	2.34	2.25	2.34	2.39
Index numbers for above	101.8	97.8	103.4	102.6	102.4	102.2
Index numbers of prices	131.2	101.4	98.5	104.3	104.3	102.4
Engineering and Construction Works						
Carpenter	2.73	2.65	2.91	2.99	3.09	2.98
Plaster	2.84	2.79	3.11	3.15	3.32	3.25
Stone-cutter	3.30	3.19	3.45	3.54	3.55	3.47
Bricklayer	3.27	3.16	3.35	3.38	3.45	3.33
Roofing-tile layer	3.11	3.05	3.50	3.60	3.72	3.44
Painter	2.55	2.44	2.67	2.76	2.86	2.85
Index numbers for above	96.5	93.0	102.3	104.2	108.0	105.2
Index numbers of prices	131.2	101.4	98.5	104.3	104.3	102.4
Total average of index numbers for all industrial workers	96.8	95.8	102.2	102.1	104.2	103.0
Index numbers of prices	131.2	101.4	98.5	104.3	104.3	102.4

[1] The average money wages contained in this table are based on the Department of Finance's *The Twenty-sixth Financial and Economic Annual of Japan for 1926*, Tokio, 1927, pp. 81-83. Index numbers are based on the Bank of Japan's wholesale price index. For both prices and wages the average of 1921-1922 is taken as 100.

With such a rise of industrialization, Japan began to have social problems of a modern type. According to Mr. C. Machita, ex-Minister of Agriculture and Forestry of the Wakatsuki cabinet, there were but 30 tenancy disputes during 1917. These increased to 1,680 disputes in 1921 and to 2,206 disputes in 1925. In 1914 we had only 50 strikes involving 8,000 industrial workers. This number of strikes increased to 333, involving 54,000 workers in 1924. Twenty years ago we had no labor union of modern type; but to-day we have more than 30 industrial labor unions with membership of a half-million workers. The labor-union movement is getting very strong in Japan, although the centralization of these unions seems at present impossible. It is, however, rather hopeful to expect their future development, as most of these unions have adopted for their tactics parliamentarism since the promulgation of manhood suffrage in 1925. Rationalization of labor seems the only solution of Japan's rapid industrialization. Japan has plenty of workers. She has an easy access to raw materials as well as markets for finished products. Japanese seamanship is not inferior to that of any Western nationals. What she lacks most is the efficiency of labor and production.

This inefficiency may not only be seen in her industry and agriculture but also in her monetary and banking systems and practices. As a result of the Chino-Japanese war in 1894-1895, and the Russo-Japanese war in 1904-1905 and rapid reorganization and improvement of society, a certain degree of inflation had been customary before the Great War. And after the War this inflation has become even greater, while the failure of big firms and banks began to be more frequent. All this indicates that there is something wrong with our monetary and banking systems as well as practices. The Japanese must admit these defects, and are better off if they face realities boldly.

3. JAPANESE MONETARY SYSTEM

The present Japanese yen is based on the Coinage Law of 1897,[1] which established the gold standard, and which definitely states that the monetary unit of Japan is 1 yen, having the weight of 2 *fun* pure gold.[2] Now 1 *fun* equals 5.78711 grains. Therefore, 2 *fun* equals 11.57422 grains. To this amount of pure gold an alloy of 1.28602 grains is added, making the total weight of 1 yen 12.86024 grains and a fineness of $\frac{11.57422}{12.86024}$ or 900 parts : 1000 parts.[3] But actually no such 1 yen goldpiece exists, for such a 1 yen goldpiece would be too small for actual purposes. The smallest piece is 5 yen, which contains 5 times 2 *fun* or 1 *momme* or 28.93555 grains of pure gold. Likewise, a 10 yen piece is 10 times, and a 20 yen piece is 20 times, 2 *fun*. Of course, these are made full legal tender. Other coins are all debased, such as silver coins of 1 yen, 50 sen, 20 sen, and 10 sen (1 sen being $\frac{1}{100}$ of 1 yen) and nickel coin of 5 sen and copper coins of 1 sen and 2 sen.

The gold coins are subject to free, unlimited and gratuitous coinage. But actually gold is not circulating; paper money is taking its place.

Besides coins, we have in circulation, since October, 1917, the Government fractional currency of 10, 20, and 50 sen denominations for the purpose of facilitating small change. The greatest medium of exchange, outside of checks, is, of course, the Bank of Japan's notes. The denominations are 1 yen, 5 yen, 10 yen, 20 yen, 50 yen, 100 yen and 200 yen.

[1] Before 1897 Japan was a bimetallism country in practice, because one yen silver coin was a legal tender, its ratio to gold being fixed at 1 : 16.014. See Japan's first modern Coinage Regulation of 1871, which went into effect after Feudalism was overthrown.

[2] Article II of the Coinage Law of 1897.

[3] Article V of the Coinage Law of 1897.

These are all convertible into gold, except 1 yen notes, which are exchangeable for silver.

The relative amounts of these media of exchange in actual circulation have been as follows:

Means of Payment in Japan
(million yen)

At the end of	*Bills* (Amount of clearance)	*Bank notes*	*Government fractional notes*	*Subsidiary coins*	[illegible]
1897	741	266	...	57	1,064
1914	10,269	385	...	140	10,794
1917	31,789	831	19	151	32,790
1921	68,201	1,546	216	205	70,168
1923	68,185	1,703	68	349	70,305
1925	83,112	1,631	18	606	85,367

In Japan relatively much more cash is needed, as retail business is carried on by cash transactions and the credit account of month-end settlements. Checks and bills are used only for wholesale and large business transactions.

Now coming back to the monetary unit. Since the Japanese yen is the unit of 11.57422 grains of pure gold and the English pound, 113.0016 grains and the American dollar, 23.22 grains, it is clear that the English pound is 9.7632 times heavier and the American dollar 2.006 times heavier than the Japanese yen. Or to state it in a technical way, mint pars of the Japanese yen in terms of these foreign monies are as follows:

For Great Britain

Great Britain ..	Gross weight of sovereign	123.27447 grains
	Less $\frac{1}{12}$ alloy	10.27287 grains
	Pure gold in sovereign	113.0016 grains
Japan	Gross weight of yen	12.86024 grains
	Less $\frac{1}{10}$ alloy	1.28602 grains
	Pure gold in yen	11.57422 grains

Therefore .....

$$1\ yen \ldots = \frac{11.57422}{113.00160} \times £1 = £0.102425 = 2/0\tfrac{9}{16}$$

$$1\ pound = \frac{113.00160}{11.57422} \times Y\ 1 = Y\ 9.7632$$

FOR U. S. A.

U. S. A.	Gross weight of dollar	25.8 grains
	Less $\frac{1}{10}$ alloy	2.58 grains
	Pure gold in dollar	23.22 grains
Japan	Pure gold in yen	11.57422

Therefore

$$1 \text{ yen} \ldots = \frac{11.57422}{23.22000} \times \$1 = \$0.49845$$

$$1 \text{ dollar} = \frac{23.22}{11.57422} \times Y\ 1 = Y\ 2.0061$$

FOR FRANCE

France	Gross weight of franc	4.9781 grains
	Less $\frac{1}{10}$ alloy	.4978 grains
	Pure gold in franc	4.4803 grains
Japan	Pure gold in yen	11.57422

Therefore

$$1 \text{ yen} \ldots = \frac{11.57422}{4.4803} \times \text{fr. } 1 = \text{fr. } 2.5833$$

$$1 \text{ franc} = \frac{4.4803}{11.57422} \times Y\ 1 = Y\ 0.38707$$

Under normal conditions this mint parity of the yen is, of course, the pivotal point around which actual exchanges cluster. The " spreads " of fluctuation are naturally limited within the specie points. To illustrate, if the yen exchange [1] is above $50.50,[2] Americans had better send gold specie instead of buying such dearer yen, for such action compensates more than the cost of shipping gold. Conversely, if the yen is below $49.125, the Japanese had better ship gold to effect payments. The specie points of yen for sovereign, franc, mark, lira and other European currencies under normal conditions are generally considered to lie somewhere

[1] By yen exchange is meant the exchange in which one side of the equation is the Japanese yen whether the method of quoting is expressed in terms of home money or foreign money.

[2] Exchange on America is quoted in Japan per 100 yen. The exact import point is somewhere between $50.3/8 and $50½, depending upon the advisability of a particular situation and its export point is likewise somewhere between $49.1/8 and $49.1/4.

between .75 per cent and 1.2 per cent premium or discount from the mint par. That is to say, if the European exchanges fall below or rise above 1.2 per cent of gold par, gold movement takes place, because the cost of shipping specie under ordinary circumstances is considered below 1.2 per cent of the total amount of such ordinary specie flow.[1]

But when we come to the Chinese or Indian exchange, the matter is a little more complicated.[2] There is no such fixed par as we find with gold countries. The price of silver fluctuates continually under the varying forces of supply and demand. The result is, the higher the price of silver, the dearer will be the tael and rupee, or vice versa. For instance, in January, 1920 the maximum price of silver in London was 85 *d.* and in New York $1.37 per ounce, and the exchange in Japan on Shanghai was 29 taels, and on Bombay 106 rupees per Y. 100 respectively. But just one year later when the price of silver went down to just one-half of the former price, taels and rupees became cheaper, and the same Y. 100 could now buy twice as many rupees and taels as a year before. Under such conditions, it is necessary to calculate in every transaction how many taels or rupees [3] a price of 1 fine ounce (480 grains) can buy. To illustrate, suppose the price of a silver bar in New York is 54c., we shall then find the price of a tael something like this:

[1] S. Y. Furuya, *Foreign Exchange*, Tokio, 1923, pp. 89, 256, 656-660.

[2] Before the War the rupee was fixed at Rs. 15 to the pound sterling or at 1*s.* 4*d.* Then the parity with Japan was Rs. 153.61 per Y. 100.00. But this was broken down by the War conditions and was officially sanctioned since Feb. 1920.

[3] The rupee is now nominally stabilized by the gold exchange system, but it still needs another way of calculation, as the English silver ounce (standard ounce) contains 444 grains and the Indian rupee 165 grains of pure silver.

(a) 1 fine ounce : fine ounces of Shanghai tael :: price of silver bar : price of Shanghai tael.

(b) 480 : 522.37[1] :: 54 : x
$x = 58.76$ (or 1 Shanghai tael = c. 58.76).

But this is only an approximate par, a par which corresponds to the mint par in gold countries. For it is nothing but a price of silver in tael, expressed in some gold money—in this case in American money. In order to get a real rate of exchange we must add to this money factor a location factor. Thus, in New York the actual rate on Shanghai may be above c. 58.76 per tael or below that price. Now if the actual rate is too high and more than compensates for the expense of shipping silver, the American will prefer to ship silver bars instead of buying such abnormally high taels, or to import silver if the tael in Shanghai is cheaper than the actual price of silver plus the expense of importation. But to the Japanese there is still another factor working in the actual calculation of the price of the tael. That factor is the exchange rate between Japan and America, if New York silver is taken into consideration. For c. 58.76 is the price of silver in New York and not in Japan. And, therefore, we are interested in finding out how much in Japanese money we can get out of this price of c. 58.76. If the Japanese-American exchange is low, more yens are needed to buv taels; if high, less yens are needed.[2]

Thus, although there is no fixed par and no fixed specie points in the Japanese-Chinese exchange, yet there is a so-called *moving par* and moving silver import and export points, by means of which we can calculate the dearness or cheapness of the Chinese exchange.

[1] Weight of the Shanghai tael. Hence, the constant number for exchange calculation for America is 108.228.

[2] This is extremely important to keep in mind when later we discuss silver exchange.

So far we have dealt with the metallic value of the yen and its corresponding external value. Our next task is to study its internal value or its purchasing power. But as the purchasing power of a money under normal conditions is more dependent on the note-issuing system and its practice than other factors, it is well here to explain briefly how the Japanese bank notes are issued, and how they circulate under ordinary circumstances.

The Bank of Japan was established in 1882, and soon assumed for itself the sole agency of note issue. The note issue system of the Bank of Japan as it stands now dates back to 1884, when the Convertible Bank Note Act was first passed. Although since then there have been three minor changes in the law, yet the main parts of the system have remained intact. The system comprises three parts. The first is the specie reserve issue. This has no limit; that is, the Bank can issue as much as it has in gold and silver. But silver must not exceed more than one-fourth of the entire conversion reserve.[1] The second is the security issue.[2] Of this the Bank is privileged to issue over the specie reserve issue up to the amount of 120 million yen, backed by such securities as government bonds, treasury notes and other bonds and commercial bills of a reliable nature. The third is known as " the excess issue ". Should it be deemed necessary on account of any extraordinary condition in the money market, the Bank may be allowed to issue more notes than what it might under the first and second methods. But for this emergency issue, the Bank is required to pay more than 5 per cent issue-tax to the Government, the exact percentage being fixed each time by the Finance Minister.[3] So

[1] But practically the Bank has no silver. All are gold coins and gold bullion. *See* Finance Dept., *Kinyu Jiko*, 1925, p. 13.

[2] For the security issue, the Bank is required to pay a tax of 1¼ per cent on the amount outstanding.

[3] At present such a tax is fixed at 6 per cent.

under ordinary circumstances, strictly speaking, the Bank of Japan has a power over the money market with its paid-up capital of 37.5 million yen and a reserve of 70.4 million yen (in 1925) and the security issue of 120 million yen, or 228 million yen in all, to act as the central bank. But the Bank's policy is such that even this small amount is not always effectively utilized to direct or control business. Their requirements for loans are too rigid. They prefer government bonds to commercial papers.

The relative amount of gold reserve in reference to other forms of reserve has been as follows:

Relative Amount of Reserves for Note Issue[1]

(million yen)

At the end of	Note issue outstanding	Gold reserve		Security Reserves				
				Gov't bonds	Other bonds	Commercial paper	Total	
		Amt.	%				Amt.	%
1897	226	98	43	55	31	41	127	57
1907	369	161	44	117	23	66	208	56
1914	385	218	57	71	77	17	167	43
1915	430	248	58	47	119	14	181	42
1916	801	410	68	37	153	..	190	32
1917	831	649	78	40	140	..	181	22
1918	1,144	712	62	40	337	53	431	38
1919	1,555	951	61	70	252	280	603	39
1920	1,439	1,246	87	92	43	56	192	13
1921	1,546	1,245	81	69	62	169	300	19
1922	1,558	1,063	68	36	212	246	494	32
1923	1,703	1,057	62	148	205	292	646	38
1924	1,662	1,059	64	145	182	274	603	36

By looking at these figures, an experienced banker may be able to tell, or at least to suspect, wherein the weakest spot

[1] These figures are compiled from the Department of Finance, *Kinyu Jikō Sankosho*, 1924, p. 13.

lies in the Japanese note-issue system which resulted in a great currency inflation. But that will be discussed later. Suffice it here to mention that the gold reserve, especially since 1914, is very high, 57 to 87 per cent, and that securities are mostly government or public bonds, and, lastly, that the security of commercial paper has been lacking, especially prior to 1918.

4. JAPANESE BANKING SYSTEM

The monetary system and the system of note issue in Japan have been briefly explained. It may be well here to insert a brief description of her banking system before we come to discuss her foreign exchange markets.

The germ of real banking in Japan is found in Osaka in the early part of the seventeenth century when such firms as Tennoji Gorobei, Kohashi Jotoku and Kagiya Rokubei began not only to accept deposits and make loans on mortgages and credits for other merchants (they themselves were big merchants as well as big money-changers) but also to finance Daimios (feudal lords of various provinces) who seemed to be short of funds even at that time. The period is marked by the vicissitudes of an inadequate coinage system, as each Daimio, having circulated his own money and bills, changed the system occasionally to serve his own interests and his domains. So in a place like Osaka where rice and other commodities were extensively marketed, various kinds of money and bills appeared which needed to be exchanged or discounted. For instance, we see that there were seven kinds of bills already used at that time.[1]

In the eighteenth and in the first part of the nineteenth century, such rice merchants were becoming big discount companies (kawase kaisha). The same conditions were also

[1] *Cf. A History of Banking in All Leading Nations* (writer, J. Soyeda), New York, 1896, vol. iv, pp. 412-3.

developing in Tokio, Yokohama, Niigata, Kyoto, Kobé, Otsu and Tsuruga.

The year 1868 saw the Restoration, and the Meiji era began with that date. But the banking and the coinage systems were still unsettled. The circulation of irregular coins with changing values, the confused state of depreciated currencies, and the lack of an organized banking system were keenly felt, especially by those people who had successfully overthrown the Tokugawa Shogunate régime and brought about a new modern state in Japan. Only two years later, in 1870, Mr. Ito (later Marquis) went to the United States to investigate the banking system of that country. The result was the adoption of the National Banks Regulations of 1872, the first banking system of modern type in Japan.

The National Banks Regulations of 1872 were patterned after the National Bank Act of U. S. A., and provided for the convertibility of the national bank notes into specie. But when the National Banks became too numerous and their notes too redundant, the desire to control them through some one central bank became very strong. To comply with this desire, in 1882 the Bank of Japan was established, as mentioned before. The next year saw an amendment to the National Banks Regulations by which the privilege of issuing notes was taken away from the national banks and granted exclusively to the newly created central Bank, and suitable measures for the redemption of the national bank notes were taken. Meanwhile, the adoption of the gold standard in 1897 systematized the monetary system in Japan, and private banks and bank-like companies which were formed under ordinary commercial law had increased in number. But some had too small capital, while others had practised methods which could not be tolerated in banks. Yet there were no general provisions to control such banks and companies beyond their subjection to the ordinary commercial or civil law under local authorities. To bring them under more efficient control and to safeguard the public, the Ordinary Banks Regulations and the Savings Banks Regulations were promulgated in 1890 and put in force three years later. Side by side with these private banks, the natinoal banks acted from the first as financial organs of general trade. When the terms of their charters expired, most of them continued business as private banks, and by February 1899, the national banks ceased to exist as such, so there was no longer any difference in economic functions and legal nature between the former national banks and private banks, all of which are now subject to the general banking laws and under the control of a Finance Minister, whose license is required for the establishment of a new bank or the amalgamation of existing banks. He is also empowered to order at any time the investigation of the business condition and property of a bank. Every bank must every half-year prepare and present to the said Minister a balance-sheet and other business reports. The former must be published in some newspaper.

In the way of bank regulation, a recent issue of Savings Banks Regulations of 1921 which was put in force after January 1, 1922 is noteworthy. Among the limitations put on the business of Savings Banks, the following are more remarkable changes: (1) savings banks shall not own or take as security for loans or deposits more than one-fifth of the total stock of a company, (2) loans to one person shall not exceed one-tenth of the total amount of the paid-up capital and reserve fund of the bank, (3) the total amount of loans on real estate mortgages shall not exceed the total amount of paid-up capital and reserve fund of the bank, (4) the total amount of deposit with any bank and of bills purchasable as accepted by the said bank shall neither exceed one-tenth of the amount of the deposits received, nor be more than one-fourth of the paid-up capital and reserve fund of the said bank, (5) and lastly, but not least important, savings banks are obliged to deposit an amount of government bonds with the Deposit Section of the Department of Finance as a guarantee for repayment of the deposits, such bonds to be not less than one-third of the deposits.

After the enactment of this law, the savings-bank failures became very much smaller in number than in former years. But ordinary banks are still free from such strict regulations. Perhaps the severest obligation now is that when a bank cannot pay its liabilities with the assets, the directors are jointly under unlimited liability as regards the deposits received before the registration of resignation, and this liability continues for two years after such resignation. But the directors could shift their property to some one else and easily evade the law. The result was actually unsatisfactory, as some bankers took advantage of the defects of the Ordinary Banks Regulations.

Aside from Ordinary Banks and Savings Banks, there sprang up since 1880, under special charters, what we call Special Banks. These are the Yokohama Specie Bank (1880), the Bank of Japan (1882), the Hypothec Bank of Japan (1897), the Bank of Taiwan (1899), the Hokkaido Colonial Bank (1899), the Industrial Bank of Japan (1902), the Bank of Chosen (1909), and the Chosen Industrial Bank (1918). Of these, the Bank of Japan has been explained elsewhere. For other special banks a few words of explanation may be necessary. The Hypothec Bank of Japan or Nippon Kangyo Ginko is the central organization for the Agricultural and Industrial Banks which are scattered all over the country. These numerous Agricultural and Industrial Banks are local financial organs for furnishing long-term loans — five to fifty years — at a low rate of interest on security of immovable property, such as, agricultural lands, forests, buildings, etc. But with a view of affording better financial facilities to local districts, a law was passed in 1921 by which the Hypothec Bank was granted the right to take over the business of the Agricultural and Industrial Banks which desire to be amalgamated under the condition that it should establish its branches in places where head offices and branches of the latter were in existence. As a result many amalgamations took place and are still taking place. In order to finance farmers and others at a low rate of interest the Hypothec Bank is authorized to issue mortgage debentures to an amount not exceeding fifteen times its paid-up capital, provided the amount of such debentures shall not exceed the total amount of outstanding loans, redeemable by annual installments or within a fixed term, and the debentures of the Agricultural and Industrial Banks, the Hokkaido Colonial Bank and the Chosen Industrial Bank the Bank has on hand. These mortgage debentures must be redeemed by means of drawings, taking place at least twice a year in amounts proportionate to the amount to be redeemed in the same year of the loans, redeemable by annual installments, with the debentures of the above-mentioned banks.

The Bank of Taiwan and the Bank of Chosen are of the same nature, the former being designated as the central bank of Taiwan and the latter as the central bank of Chosen with the note-issuing power. The system of note issue is something like that of the Bank of Japan, the security issue being limited to 20 million yen for the former and 50 million yen for the latter. But since the Great War the actual circulation under the security issue has been 30 to 40 million yen for the Taiwan, and 60 to 160 million yen for the Chosen. The Bank of Chosen notes since November, 1917 were also proclaimed to be the sole legal tender throughout Kwantung Province and the South Manchurian Railway Zone, and as a result thereof all the Yokohama Specie Bank's gold notes then circulating in Manchuria were to be gradually replaced by the Bank of Chosen notes.

The Hokkaido Colonial Bank and the Chosen Industrial Bank were established with the object of supplying capital for colonizing and exploiting Hokkaido by the former and Chosen by the latter.

These last-named four banks were recklessly expanding credits during and after the War, extending loans twice as much as deposits and seven times as much as their paid-up capital and reserve.[1] After 1920 they were many times in financial difficulties and have been saved by the Bank of Japan.

The Industrial Bank of Japan or Nippon Kogyo Ginko is a joint-stock company whose chief object is to finance ship-building companies and other industrial enterprises of urban districts, and to subscribe for or take up national and local bonds and companies' debentures, etc. The Bank is also authorized for these purposes to issue debentures to an amount not exceeding ten times its paid-up capital, provided, however, the amount of such debentures shall not exceed the total amount of outstanding loans, discounted bills, and national or local bonds, companies' debentures and shares, and gold and silver bullion in hand.

The growth of these Special Banks may be seen by the following statistics.

Since the Agricultural and Industrial Banks are for the benefit of farmers, and other Special Banks and Ordinary Banks are for the use of industrialists and merchants, Mutual Loan Societies or Mujin exist for the mutual protection of peasants, for peasants have nothing to offer as mortgages; hence banks are of little use to them. The object of the Mujin

[1] *See* statistics in Department of Finance, *Kinyu Jiko Sankosho*, Tokio, 1924, pp. 71, 94-99.

GROWTH OF SPECIAL BANKS[1]

(million yen)

	At the Time of Establishment		In 1923			
	Authorized Capital	Paid up Capital	Authorized Capital	Paid up Capital	Reserve	Dividend
Bank of Japan (1882)	10	2.	60	37.5	58.8	12%
Yokohama Specie Bank (1880)	3	1.4	100	100.	77.1	12%
Hypothec Bank of Japan (1897)	10	2.5	94	69.8	26.8	10%
Bank of Taiwan (1899)	5	1.25	60	52.5	12.9	7%
Hokkaido Colonial Bank (1899)	3	.75	20	12.5	4.6	10%
Industrial Bank of Japan (1902)	10	2.5	50	50.	15.	10%
Bank of Chosen (1909)	10	2.5	80	59.	11.	6%

is to collect a small sum of money, say once a month, from all members of the society, and to loan the sum usually without interest to the one who is in greatest need, but after the second installment the borrower is chosen by bidding the amount of interest he is willing to pay. The Mujin has existed since the thirteenth century, but as an organization of purely mutual aid it developed and flourished at the end of Tokugawa régime and the beginning of the present era. Then, the Mujin became a commercial enterprise as everything else became business enterprise. To-day they are more like peasant-banks. When regulations to control them became necessary, a law was passed in June, 1915. The development of the Mujin after that date may be seen below.

[1] These figures are based on Department of Finance, *ibid.*, pp. 71-73.

DEVELOPMENT OF MUTUAL LOAN SOCIETIES [1]

(in thousand yen)

	No. of Head Office	Branches	Authorized Capital	Paid-up Capital	Average Authorized Capital per Society
1916	136	60	7,406	2,576	54
1919	206	61	10,379	4,109	50
1923	219	45	15,014	6,501	68
1925 Joint stock companies	193	..	21,217	8,962	
1925 Limited partnerships	23	..	868	402	
1925 Ordinary partnerships	2	..	70	37	
1925 Individuals	24	..	232	232	
Total	240	..	22,386	9,635	93

Next in importance is the Postal Savings Bank. Although the post-office savings account is not quite a bank in function, as it does not make loans, yet its function as a saving depository for the lower classes of people is quite remarkable. The post-office savings first started in 1874. The interest paid by the post office has been somewhat lower than the interest paid by banks,[2] but as they specialized in deposits of small sums, refusing to receive more than 1,000 yen from any person at one time, thus making themselves accessible for the great mass of people, the growth of their deposits is certainly remarkable.

[1] These figures are made up from Department of Finance, *ibid.*, p. 102 and *The Twenty-six Financial and Economic Annual of Japan for 1926*, Tokio, 1926, p. 136.

[2] Since 1915 up to 1923 they paid interest of 4.8 per cent for deposits and after 1923 4.95 per cent whereas banks were paying 6 to 7 per cent.

Growth of Deposits of Postal Savings[1]
(in millions of yen)

	Number of Depositors	Amount of Deposits	Population	Amount of deposit per one depositor	Amount of deposit per one person
1897	1	26	43	20.94	.60
1902	2	30	46	10.44	.66
1907	7	91	48	11.67	1.87
1912	12	197	51	15.96	3.79
1917	16	416	53	24.59	7.70
1921	25	906	56	56.22	16.00

Since 1921 the growth has been even more rapid as the repeated bank failures turned the people more to the post-office. At the end of 1926 they had over 1,200 million yen in deposits. These huge sums are being utilized by the Deposit Section of the Department of Finance. But as there is practically no regulation as to the use of these funds, except that they should be invested in some public securities and bonds, the funds were not really well used, and the Deposit Section has been the target of severe criticism. It was only a few years ago that the section began to publish its financial statements for the general public.

The development of ordinary banks is also interesting. Up to the War the number of banks (head offices) or branches was not increasing; but after the War, as the capital and reserves of these banks were generally too small, the government took measures to encourage the amalgamation and affiliation of minor banks with a view to solidifying their financial ability. As the result of these efforts there have been many amalgamations and affiliations during the last several years. According to the report of the Depart-

[1] The population in this table is that of the Birth Registry, or it represents the static population. The other data are based on Department of Finance, *ibid.*, p. 23.

ment of Finance there have been 552 ordinary banks which have amalgamated and dissolved in the last 14 years, the details of which may be seen below.

BANK AMALGAMATION IN JAPAN, 1913-1926

	New Banks			Dissolution because of Amalgamation			
	Ordinary Banks	Savings Banks	Total	Ordinary Banks	Savings Banks	Others	Total
1913	3	2	5	4	..	1	5
1914	3	3	6	2	4	..	6
1915	2	2	4	2	2	..	4
1916	8	2	10	8	2	1	11
1917	13	4	17	17	4	1	22
1918	25	8	33	19	12	3	34
1919	31	19	50	35	23	8	66
1920	22	16	38	31	14	7	52
1921	39	18	57	39	29	3	71
1922	51	4	55	46	12	4	62
1923	66	1	67	88	4	5	97
1924	48	1	49	53	1	7	61
1925	69	..	69	93	2	1	96
1926	84	2	86	115	3	3	121
Total....	464	82	546	552	112	44	708

Due to these amalgamations, although the percentage of paid-up capital to authorized capital remains nearly the same, being 60 to 70 per cent on the average, yet the percentage of reserve to paid-up capital increased from an average of 30 to 40 per cent. Expenses are also greatly cut down and their financial power greatly strengthened. Deposits are also growing. On the side of advances, however, loans still occupy the greater portion, or nearly 80 per cent of the total advances, discounts being only about 15 per cent. This is perhaps the most important point to notice in Japan's banking today. For there are as yet not many negotiable bills, and what few bills are found are mostly promissory notes.

Now, it is evident that bankers neither can discount such bills nor invest in long-term industrial enterprises. Naturally they prefer loans on mortgages, bonds and stocks. But they find difficulty in making short-term investments. Bonds yield only 5 to 6 per cent. Some stocks yield 12 to 15 per cent dividend, but they are not reliable. In between them there are not many good stocks nor any amount of commercial negotiable instruments. Railways, tramways, gas, water, and the like are nearly all government or public enterprises in Japan. Under such circumstances the call-loan market is the only reservoir through which bankers finance their short-term money. For this reason alone, the bank amalgamation has proved to be a wise measure. The following statistics will show some of these tendencies.

DEVELOPMENT OF ORDINARY BANKS [1]
(million yen)

	No. of banks (head office)	Authorized Capital	Paid-up Capital	Reserve Fund	Deposits	Advances		
						Loans	Bills Discounted	Total
1897	1223	224	147	13	207	241	..	241
1907	1658	410	286	84	944	514	597	1,113
1915	1442	513	357	127	1,699	645	1,057	1,703
1925	1585	2,426	1,504	606	8,379	6,936	1,350	8,487

Under such a condition of loose bank regulation with practically no *real* supervision, no fluid market for short-time investments, over-expansion of credits during the War and up to 1920, too "isolated policy" on the part of individual bankers, no centralized banking either in the way of cash reserve or the rate of interest, scarcely any logical re-

[1] The Department of Finance, *Kinyu Jiko Sankosho*, 1924, pp. 75, 81-82, and *The Twenty-Six Financial and Economic Annual of Japan*, 1926, pp. 135-137.

adjustment after the depression of 1920, with swindles by the directors of banks such as the Seventy-fourth Bank and Mogi & Co. of Yokohama in May, 1920, the Kochi Commercial Bank and Ishii & Co. of Osaka, and the Kyoto Sekizen Bank and its directors—under such conditions—bank failures of recent years were but logical consequences. Ex-Finance Minister J. Inoue reported at the time of his writing in 1925 that there were 57 bank failures since 1920.[1] If we add more recent bank failures, especially those of March, April, 1927, this number may be easily increased to 100. The Japanese may not be particularly incapable of handling money, but rather they are the victims of *unorganized* banking due to the sudden increase of finance capital. The time has now come to correct these shortcomings, for committees of Financial Reorganization have been already appointed and a radical reform of the banking system is now under contemplation.[2] While their workings are not yet known, their objectives must be along the following lines: (1) to unify the banking system; (2) to bring it under some regulatory authority, but free from party politics; (3) to make provision for the development of a discount market; (4) to create an elastic currency; (5) to give the Bank of Japan the power to control the money market, and through the money market the business of the country.

5. FOREIGN EXCHANGE MARKETS

In our country there is no one city that can be called the New York or London of Japan. The business of the exchange markets is equally divided between Yokohama and Kobe, and, in a lesser degree, Tokio and Osaka.

[1] J. Inoue, *Japan's Financial and Economic Conditions after the War*, Tokio, 1925, p. 91.

[2] A partially reformed bank bill was passed this March, 1927. According to it, the ordinary banks hereafter must have at least Y 1,000,000 capital (and in cities Y 2,000,000) and ¼ must be paid-up.

In early days, Japan's foreign trade was carried on almost exclusively by the foreigners residing in Japan. And, therefore, it is natural that foreign exchange business was also in the hands of Dutch, British and other foreign bankers. Only a small part was transacted by the Japanese concerns which then happened to be big money exchangers. It was not until 1872, when the Government promulgated the National Bank Regulations, that Japan saw the advent of the first modern banking system. The first Japanese exchange bank was established in 1880 when the Yokohama Specie Bank came into existence under a special charter from the Government, but formed as a private corporation. Soon after the establishment of the Yokohama Specie Bank, numerous other exchange banks came into existence. In 1882 we saw the Bank of Japan formed as the central bank, one of its aims being to assist the foreign exchange banks, especially the Yokohama Specie Bank. In 1897 the Japan Hypothec Bank, in 1899 the Hokkaido Colonial Bank, and the Bank of Taiwan, in 1902 the Japan Industrial Bank, in 1909 the Bank of Chosen, came into existence. All of these are semi-public banks, but they handle foreign exchanges also. Especially, the Banks of Chosen and Taiwan deal with foreign exchange quite extensively. Meanwhile, numerous private banks such as Mitsui, Mitsubishi, Dai-ichi, Sumitomo, Yasuda, Jugo, Daiyako and others were established,[1] and have opened for-

[1] These are generally regarded as the first-rate banks. Their capitals, reserves, and deposits in millions of yen are as following: (*Japan Year Book*, 1926, p. 402).

	(million yen)		
	Paid up Capital	*Reserve*	*Deposit*
Mitsui Banks	60	52	443
Mitsubishi Bank	30	21	303
Dai-ichi Bank	50	44	359
Sumitoma Bank	50	21	373
Yasuda Bank	92	51	589
Jugo Bank	49	30	351
Dai-hyaku Bank	17	10	120

eign departments to deal in foreign exchange business, with their own foreign branches and foreign correspondents abroad. The Yokohama Specie Bank alone has at present 39 branches and 2 sub-branches, besides their foreign correspondents, scattered all over the world. Perhaps the locations of these branches indicate indirectly somewhat the sphere of Japanese trade and exchange interests.

THE YOKOHAMA SPECIE BANK, LTD.

(CAPITAL PAID UP Y 100,000,000; RESERVES Y 83,500,000)

HEAD OFFICE, YOKOHOMA.

Branches:

Japan: Kobe, Nagasaki, Nagoya, Osaka, Shimonoseki, Tokio.

China: Tsinan, Hankow, Peking, Shanghai, Tientsin, Tsingtau, Canton.

Manchuria: Changchun, Dairen, Harbin, Kaiynan, Mukden, Neuchwang.

Europe: Hamburg, London, Lyons.

North America: New York, San Francisco, Seattle, Los Angeles.

South America: Buenos Aires, Rio de Janeiro.

Others: Batavia, Bombay, Calcutta, Hongkong, Honolulu, Manila, Rangoon, Saigon, Singapore, Sourabaya, Sydney, Vladivostok, Semarang.

Along with these Japanese exchange banks we also have the foreigners' branch banks. Toward the end of the last century there were less than 10, but in 1909 there were 15, and in 1924, 22. These are British, American, Dutch, French, German, Russian and Chinese. These branch banks, however, have had no such difficulties in conducting their banking business in Japan as most of the foreign branch banks in the United States are now encountering on account of discriminatory state laws.[1]

[1] Willis and Edwards, *Banking and Business*, New York, 1925 ed., p. 281; also Willis and Steiner, *Federal Reserve Banking Practice*, New York, 1926, p. 552.

Besides bankers, exchange dealers in Japan are also bill brokers and exchange brokers. These are about sixty houses each. But bill brokers in Japan are more interested in bonds and stocks than exchanges, while exchange brokers are primarily interested in broking exchange bills and in dealing in futures.

The aggregate amount of foreign exchange bills cleared through these Japanese and foreign banks may be considered roughly 7 billion yen annually. The figures for 1925, for instance, may be calculated as follows:

Imports and Exports	Y. 4,876 million
Gold	22 "
Invisible trade	960 "
Capital movement	1,121 "
	Y. 6,979 million

But it is said that the Yokohama Specie Bank alone handles more than 50 per cent of the total of such exchange bills.[1] These are merely figures accompanied of the actual business transactions. The amounts of pure exchange speculations are not known, but are generally considered enormous.

Now the exchange rates in Japan are, of course, determined primarily at the juncture of supply and demand of exchange bills. But the fact that the Yokohama Specie Bank is the greatest buyer and seller of exchanges (besides having a special financial aid from the Bank of Japan and the Government), enables its rates to dominate the market. The Bank, having received exchange news from all important parts of the world, determines its own rates every day on foreign countries, and publishes them, and circulates them simultaneously in Yokohama, Tokio, Kobe, Osaka and other cities. Meanwhile, other bankers are adjusting their rates to the Yokohama Specie Bank rates, while exchange brokers

[1] K. Maeda, *A Study of Yen Exchange*, Tokio, 1925, p. 57.

are busily engaged in broking exchange bills, in dealing in futures and arbitraging exchanges by visiting from bank to bank, from merchant to merchant, and by means of telephone calls. Thus the exchange brokers are good levelers of exchange rates in Japan.

In general, the exchange markets are becoming more and more competitive, as the volume of trade and facilities of exchange increase. This can well be seen by the narrowing of exchange "points". In earlier days 1 "point" in Japanese British exchange was 1/4 of 1 penny, and in Japanese-American exchange 1/4 of 1 cent. But today we have 1/16 of 1 penny for the former and 1/8 of 1 cent for the latter. Exchange bills used are also numerous, ranging from the banker's clean bill to the merchant's D.P. bill. In general, documentary bills are of 30, 40, 60 days usance, while domiciled bills are still numerous, although yen bills are already introduced and used more in the Oriental trade. But owing to the absence of a discount market, the development of yen bills belongs to the future.

6. FINANCING FOREIGN TRADE

In the first place, it is extremely important at the outset to keep in mind that there is no discount market in Japan. What were called "stamped bills" at the time when Mr. J. Inoue was the Governor of the Bank of Japan, in 1919, were only used as a temporary measure. Such bills had practically gone out of circulation when the panic of 1920 came.[1]

But while there is no general market for discounting foreign exchange bills,[2] the Bank of Japan has assumed, single-handed and sometimes almost heroically, the whole responsibility for financing exports and imports, through either

[1] Toyotaro Yuki, "Why no discount market in Japan," *The Kokumin Shimbun*, Jan. 20, 21, 22, 1927.

[2] In fact there is no general market for any kind of bills.

discounting bills directly or indirectly by buying and selling foreign exchange funds. The Bank has especially helped the Yokohama Specie Bank in financing the foreign trade, and has let the Yokohama Specie Bank finance the traders directly, details of which will be fully discussed later. But suffice it here to say that there is in Japan no fluid market that would help the banks to finance such trade. So each bank has to take care of itself. The central bank is seated too far away to be reached by ordinary exchange banks. The so-called gold funds kept by the Japanese Government and the Bank of Japan in London and New York are used to peg exchanges, to keep and stabilize Japanese bonds, and to redeem and pay foreign obligations.

Briefly, such is the foreign exchange mechanism working under ordinary conditions. Let us now see, in the next chapter, how this mechanism has survived these past fourteen years under a different set of circumstances.

CHAPTER II

Japanese Yen Exchange Before 1914

I. JAPANESES EXCHANGE BEFORE 1914

While this survey devotes itself chiefly to the nature and causes of the movements of the Japanese yen exchange during the period from 1914 to 1917, it will help to a better understanding if a brief outline of yen exchange before that date be given.

The fluctuations of yen exchange before 1914 were, generally speaking, small, and its general movement was rather smooth.[1] During the time of the Russo-Japanese war, 1904-5, rather wide fluctuations took place, but their "spreads" and their effects on people when compared with those of the recent fluctuations of 1923-4 were almost negligible. The trade balance had been mostly unfavorable,[2] while invisible trade was not yet developed. And the foreign debts, particularly after the war of 1904-5, increased by leaps and bounds. The failure of Japan to get 2 billion yen war-indemnity from Russia and the subsequent increase

[1] Department of Finance, *Kinyu Jikō Sankosho*, 1924, pp. 125-6.

[2] The excess of imports was as follows: (Trade includes Chosen and Taiwan.) (In million yen.)

	Exports	*Imports*	*Excess of imports*
1897	175	231	56
1902	272	281	9
1907	442	505	63
1912	547	664	117
1913	650	778	127

of the navy and army and the building of public utilities caused her to borrow heavily from Europe. The net total borrowing in 1902, for instance, was 194 million yen, or five times that of 1897; while in 1907 it increased up to 1,400 million yen, or again increased seven-fold in five years. Such borrowing in 1913 was 1,969 million yen; [1] a country with such heavy borrowing abroad naturally had bad conditions at home, for at least one-half [2] of the borrowing was spent for

[1] The increase of Japan's foreign borrowing before 1914 may be summed up as follows: (See *Kinyu Jikō*, 1924, p. 26.) (million yen.)

JAPAN'S FOREIGN BORROWING BEFORE 1914
(Figures show amounts outstanding at the end of each year)

	Gov't foreign bonds	Domestic bonds sold abroad	Domestic bonds shipped abroad	Municipal bonds	Corporation bonds	Foreigners investment in Japan	Total
1897	..	43	..	..	..	..	43
1902	97	93	..	4	..	..	194
1907	1,165	93	57	21	44	17	1,400
1912	1,427	..	72	177	147	29	1,854
1913	1,524	..	74	177	166	26	1,969

[2] For instance, if we classify all the national debts—including domestic loans which amounts to little more than half of the total amount—since the Restoration of 1868 up to the end of December 1904, according to the objects for which they were raised, we get the following: (Figures based on *The National Debts of Japan*, by Department of Finance, Tokio, 1906, pp. 12-14.)

A. For reorganization of public institutions		Y. 225 million
For military affairs		227
Non-economic borrowing		452
B. For economic undertakings	Y. 170 million	
For financial adjustment	203	
For exploitation of new territory	27	
Economic borrowing	400	

Or again at the end of 1913, Japan's total outstanding National Debts

unproductive purposes, such as reorganization of the state, national protection, etc.

While not all borrowing was employed for productive purposes, a greater part was utilized simultaneously as a fund to peg Japanese exchanges. That is to say, any excess of credit, after debts had been paid out of a fresh foreign borrowing, was utilized as an exchange gold fund, and was kept at a foreign money center. If the fund was exhausted, it was replenished by another borrowing. But such a practice was not welcomed by the Japanese. So each government in power had adopted the so-called traditional policy of encouragement of exports and repression of imports in order to balance the payments. But the trade was not so favorable as was expected. Besides, the government kept on borrowing abroad for various purposes at home. So the government had still to peg the exchanges. And the exchange funds were aways draining away [1] in spite of this continuous borrowing.

may be divided as follows: (Figures based on Dr. U. Kobayashi, *War and Armament Loans of Japan*, New York, 1922, pp. 94-5.)

(million yen)

For economic purposes		*For non-economic purposes*	
1. Loans for reorganization of certain institutions ..	Y. 3	1. Loans for war	Y. 1,454
2. Loans for railway	796	2. Loans for armament ...	63
3. Loans for exploitation of new territory	80		1,517
4. Loans for financial adjustment	344	Total loans	Y. 2,743
	1,223		

In 1895 Japan received from China a war indemnity of 230 million taels (£38,000,000), and this she kept at London in order to meet the impending redemption of her war loans and for the purchase of ships, munitions and for other purposes. But fortunately this method of clearing international indebtedness proved to be expedient in the course of subsequent years in maintaining the value of the yen, when Japan was

Each year's successive excess of imports may have been due to many causes, but the most dominant and powerful cause, at least after the Russo-Japanese war, was the higher level of prices in Japan relative to other countries. For illustration, let us compare prices in Japan and in the United States before 1914.

	Japan	*U. S. A.*	
1900	100[1]	(110.5)[2]	100
1902	97	(112.9)	102.1
1907	129	(129.5)	117.1
1912	132	(133.6)	120.9
1913	132	(135.4)	122.5

Thus, prices in Japan were much higher than in the United States during the period 1900-1914, and since prices in

but little known to the world. (See M. Matsukata, *Report on the Adoption of Gold Standard in Japan*, Tokio, 1899, pp. 166-9). So this temporary measure remained intact and became firmly established, especially after the war with Russia (1904-5), when Japan kept practically all her foreign loans in the hands of British bankers. Following are the figures. Notice the gradual decline in the amount of the gold fund kept abroad. (Department of Finance, *Kinyu Jikō*, 1923, p. 67.)

(In millions of yen)

At the end of	Gold fund kept abroad		Gold kept at home		Total stock of gold
	Amount	%	Amount	%	
1905	442	92	36	8	479
1907	401	90	44	10	445
1910	336	70	135	30	471
1911	231	63	132	37	364
1912	214	62	136	38	350
1913	246	65	130	35	376

[1] This is the Bank of Japan's index number of wholesale prices, Oct. 1900 = 100.

[2] U. S. wholesale prices, 1890-99 = 100. Calculated from Edwin R. A. Seligman, *Principles of Economics*, 1926 ed., pp. 466-7.

Great Britain were much below the American prices during those years,[1] Japanese prices must have been very much higher than those of the British. Of course, one may distrust index numbers of this kind, especially those compiled by the Bank of Japan. But apart from certain technical errors, what is emphasized here is not so much the relative heights of the two indices at a given month or year as the general trend or movement of prices throughout a period of years. In this sense, Japanese prices were moving relatively at a faster rate than the British or the American.

Now, a critical reader may ask, what were the causes for such high prices? The answer is, surely not the exchange rates. Exchanges were pegged nearly at par. And what "unfavorable" exchanges there were, were very slight, even if they had acted to some extent as cause. But again, among other causes, the most dominant was the undue expansion of note-issue. This was undue expansion because, among the specie reserves against which the Bank of Japan issued notes, was included the stock of gold the Bank borrowed abroad. To illustrate, in 1907 the specie reserve for the note-issue was 161 million yen, but the same government statistics show that there were only 44 million yen gold at home and 401 million yen abroad. Therefore, even if all of this 44 million yen belonged to the Bank of Japan alone (in fact, some belonged to the government), the Bank must have utilized at least 117 million yen of gold abroad for note-issuing purposes at home. This practice had a most disastrous effect on prices and trade, because the expansion of note-issue due to the increase in foreign reserve was (1) enormous in quantity,[2] and (2) the expansion was not due

[1] *See* Chart in Seligman's *ibid.*, pp. 466-7.

[2] This point will be more fully discussed later. But here we are only concerned with the period from the time of the Russo-Japanese war to

to the demand of business but rather to the government's fiscal needs such as in military expansion and social reorganization.[1] This malpractice of issuing notes against foreign funds was kept up during the Great War and throughout the panic of 1920 and up to September 1922, when the then existing cabinet finally abolished it.

A critical reader may still ask at this point, why was it that relatively high prices in Japan caused her to have an unfavorable balance of payments? Are not the Japanese commodities different from those of Westerners? Should not, therefore, the comparison of prices be limited to those of international commodities that are subject to international

the World War. (Department of Finance, *Kinyu Jikō Sankosho for 1924*, Government Printing Office, Tokio, 1925, pp. 10-11, 67-69.)

(million yen)

End of	Note-issue: Gold Reserve	Note-issue: Security Reserve	Note-issue: Total	Total gold at home	Total gold held abroad	Therefore Amount of gold abroad utilized for note-issue
1907	161	208	369	44	401	117
1912	247	201	448	136	215	111
1913	224	202	426	130	246	94

Dr. U. Kobayashi of Meiji University has admirably brought out in his book the rise of prices in Japan due to wars and armament, but unfortunately he failed *to connect* such foreign loans to the over-issue of bank notes in Japan. To quote his words, "In short, the excess of importation and efflux of specie from the Restoration (1868) until 1881 were occasioned by the over-issue of inconvertible paper money... from Sino-Japanese war...and through Russo-Japanese war...up to 1912...the excess of importation and the outflow of specie was wholly due to war loans and conversion loans...There is no doubt that these appreciations were due to the inflation of currency which, in turn, was brought about by the increased issue of paper money and convertible notes in connection with the war." Dr. U. Kobayashi, *War and Armament Loans of Japan*, New York, 1922, p. 196.

movements? My answer is, no. Japan is very much dependent on her foreign trade. The character of her foreign trade is such that the prices of purely domestic goods such as *miso* and *shoyu,* for which the Westerners have no equivalents, do constitute some of the important elements in the cost of living, and do influence greatly the cost of export goods. To illustrate, raw silk which constitutes 32 to 44 per cent of the total exports and nearly 90 per cent of which come to America depends for its cost of production mainly upon the cost of living or, to be more specific, the general level of prices. The same thing can be said about her exports of cotton goods, knitted goods, etc., although in these cases raw materials must be first imported before manufacture. In the long run, therefore, the domestic price situation affects greatly Japan's balance of payments.

To sum up, prices in Japan after the Russo-Japanese war were relatively higher than those of America or Great Britain. This was mainly due to great expenditures in her national reorganization. In order to meet this expenditure, she sacrificed to adopt a sound monetary policy. And each year saw an unfavorable balance of trade. Specie went out of the country. Yen exchanges naturally tended to go down, but were actually held up by the system of gold exchange funds. Japan's invisible trade was not yet developed, and her chief importation of capital arose from the government's borrowing abroad.

CHAPTER III

Yen Exchange and the Balance of Payments During the War, 1914-1918

I. THE HISTORY OF YEN EXCHANGE CLASSIFIED INTO THREE PERIODS

In the various accompanying charts the general movement of Japanese yen exchange during 1914 to 1927 will be shown. In these charts I have deliberately chosen three exchanges—New York, London and Shanghai—as the representative exchanges in Japan to show the general trend of the yen exchange movement. The exchanges on New York and on London in Japan are the most important; they have been the barometer of the value of the Japanese yen, for nearly all of Japan's external trade and finances are transacted either in sterling or dollar exchange. On the other hand, Shanghai exchange is a good representative of the silver exchanges, for Japan's trade with China is next important to the trade with the United States in amount; besides, it indicates the general trend of silver exchanges whereby Japan has to deal with silver Oriental countries.

The trends of these exchanges can be divided into the following three periods:

1. The First period, 1914-1918.
2. The Second period, 1919-1923.
3. The Third period, 1924-1927.

The reason for so classifying is because in each of these periods we find the exchanges operated under a set of different forces. The first period was characterized by the war conditions; the second by peace but much disturbed and maladjusted conditions; the third by the great earthquake. Speaking of the yen exchange movement itself, the first is the period of strong exchange; the second is the period of weak exchange; and the third, the period of slumps.

This chapter is devoted to the first period, a period of war—of strong exchange during 1914-1918.

2. ECONOMIC CONDITIONS UP TO JULY 1914

As was explained in the preceding chapter, Japan's economic position before the War was truly that of a debtor country. Her imports were increasing more rapidly than her exports; and each year this excess of imports took the form of foreign loans, and foreign loans in turn caused more imports. To illustrate by the year 1913, our commodity exports were 650 million yen and our commodity imports were 778 million yen, making a total trade deficit of 127 million yen.[1] The situation was not only bad in commodity trade but also in invisible trade. For Japan this year owed to foreign countries more than 1,969 million yen loans, interest of which alone would have been more than 130 million yen. Over against these foreign debts, our only credit was Chinese loans and investments, which amounted roughly to 400 million yen, and the freight receipts, which have been the chief source of Japan's invisible trade, netted her only 40 million yen. All other incomes—such as insurance premiums, immigrants' remittances, profits by the Japanese — all combined—would not have reduced this interest of 130 million yen to nil. In fact, in the invisible trade items, Japan made a deficit to the amount of 13 million yen.[2] In order to offset

[1] The figures include Chosen and Taiwan. Hereafter the same statistics are used unless otherwise specified as Japan proper.

[2] J. Inoue, *Japan's International Finance after the War*, Tokio, 1925, Appendix vii.

this 13 million yen and the above deficit of commodity trade of 127 million yen, Japan borrowed 116 million yen abroad and shipped out net 26 million yen worth of gold and silver in 1913.

Such a state of deficit settlement was grievous. So when the Okuma cabinet came into power in April, 1914, its first task was not to borrow any more capital but to encourage exports and repress imports. Now in order to carry out this traditional policy of encouragement of exports and repression of imports, it was thought that there were two means. One was to encourage trade and industries by giving trade information and reports to merchants and manufacturers and by establishing such trade aid organizations as the Imperial Raw Silk Association. The other was to control the yen exchange through the Yokohama Specie Bank so that exporters could always command better prices for their export bills and importers would have to pay higher prices for their import bills. That is to say, the government let the Yokohama Specie Bank maintain rates one or two points always lower than those of foreign branch bankers in Japan. For this purpose the government has been advancing to the Yokohama Specie Bank through the Bank of Japan an exchange capital to the amount of 20 million yen at a lower rate of interest.[1] The result was that more export bills were coming to the Yokohama Specie Bank, since the Japanese exporters could realize more yen by selling their dollar or sterling bills at lower rates of exchange. But importers were less encouraged to deal at such unfavorable rates. So they had either to curtail their imports or to buy cheaper foreign money from the foreign branch bankers in order to pay off their bills.[2] This policy, however, was not success-

[1] S. Y. Furuya, *Foreign Exchange*, Tokio, 1923, p. 630; K. Maeda, *A Study of Yen Exchange*, p. 57.

[2] To illustrate, suppose that the Bank's selling rate for demand drafts

ful. Prices declined a little but not much, and the excess of imports still continued. At this time the War broke out. The War proved to be the rescuer of Japan so far as her financial and trade situations were concerned.

3. CHANGES BROUGHT BY THE WAR IN THE BALANCE OF PAYMENTS

So far as it concerned Japan's economic relations to the world, the War brought to her four fundamental changes. (A) The first was the change on her commodity trade. The nature of Japan's trade had been completely changed when her succession of over-imports was reversed to a succession of over-exports. (B) The second was the change in her invisible trade. Like the visible trade, her invisible account has been changed from a debit to a credit balance. This was largely due to the increase of her merchant marine and decrease in her foreign loans. (C) Still the third change was brought about when her international and financial position was elevated from that of debtor nation to that of creditor nation. (D) The fourth was the change in the yen exchange situation. Her yen exchange was no longer the object to be feared. In fact, the yen exchange had remained the most stabilized exchange among the belligerent countries throughout the War.[1]

on New York was \$48.00 (per Y. 100.00), the Bank's buying rate for the exporter's bill of 4 months would be \$49.⅜. For the difference between \$48.00 and \$49.⅜ or \$1.⅜ would be the interest on Y. 100.00 for 4 months which corresponds roughly to 6.6% interest. Now, if the Bank reduces this buying rate to \$48.⅜, the American importer pays just as much money as before, say \$100.00, but the Japanese exporter can now realize Y. 206.71, whereas formerly he could get only Y. 202.53. But if the Bank reduces \$1.00 of its buying rate, it would also reduce its selling rate by \$1.00, making the rate at \$47.00. So the importer by the same reason but worked out conversely has to pay more or else to curtail his imports.

[1] This can be seen in various charts prepared by Federal Reserve *Bulletin*, September 1918, pp. 937-8, and November 1920, p. 1159.

But the change in exchange was more than that. The importance held by the sterling exchange in Japan was soon replaced by the dollar exchange. And the whole system of exchange was adjusted accordingly.

For these great changes a little more elucidation is necessary. Let us first review her trade expansion. Prices were now becoming relatively high abroad (see the next chart) and demand was persistent because of the war. In those five years of war, Japan could net in her favor more than 1,566 million yen in commodity trade. Figures may be seen below.

JAPAN'S COMMODITY TRADE DURING THE WAR [1]
(million yen)

Year	*Exports*	*Imports*	*Excess*	*4% Correction* [2]	*Total excess*
1914	609	632	-23	25	2
1915	732	562	169	22	191
1916	1,172	973	379	38	417
1917	1,662	1,087	575	43	618
1918	2,012	1,742	269	69	339
					1,566

With such heavy exports, Japan was naturally piling up gold exchange funds in New York and London. Demand for bills to get these funds was far outbalanced by the immense supply of bills to claim more funds in these centers.

[1] These figures include Chosen and Taiwan. Department of Finance, *Kinyu Jikō Sankosho*, 1924, p. 219.

[2] Since 1899 Japan's exports have been calculated from f. o. b. prices, whereas her imports have been calculated from c. i. f. prices. In order to correct the figures, it is claimed by the officials of the Department of Finance that 4 per cent of total imports should be subtracted from such import figures. *See* also H. Kashiwagi, "The Japanese Yen and Japan's Economic Condition," *The Foreign Securities Investor*, March 31, 1926, p. 4. Others like ex-Finance Minister Wakatsuki in the Katsura Cabinet and ex-Professor H. Tsumura of Kobe Commercial College claim that at least 12 to 20 per cent should be readjusted. But in this survey the former conservative view is adopted.

Under such one-sided conditions, foreign money was getting cheaper, and the value of yen was getting higher. Because of this high rate of yen exchange foreign countries, especially the United States until she put an embargo on gold in September 7, 1917, were shipping gold to Japan to offset their payments. The total net import of such gold and silver into Japan for the period was 274 million yen.[1] Therefore, if we subtract this amount from the total excess of commodity exports, we still get a net real balance of trade of 1,292 million yen.

JAPAN'S VISIBLE TRADE DURING THE WAR

(million yen)

	1914	*1915*	*1916*	*1917*	*1918*	*Total*
Total excess of exports	2	191	417	618	338	1,566
Net gold and silver imports	20	20	−72	−238	−4	−274
Total visible trade balance	22	211	345	380	334	1,292

The above trade figures show that, although imports were very much increased, yet the increase of exports was far greater. This enormous increase of exports was due to the war needs and the high prices abroad. It was not due to

[1] Japan imported gold and silver a great deal from U. S. A. but reshipped them to India and China in order to settle the account with these countries. Gold movement for the period was as follows: (Department of Finance, *Kinyu Jikō*, 1925, pp. 233-240).

JAPAN'S GOLD AND SILVER MOVEMENT DURING THE WAR

(million yen)

	Exports	*Imports*	*Excess*
1914	29	9	20
1915	44	24	20
1916	28	101	−72
1917	153	392	−238
1918	1	5	−4
			−274

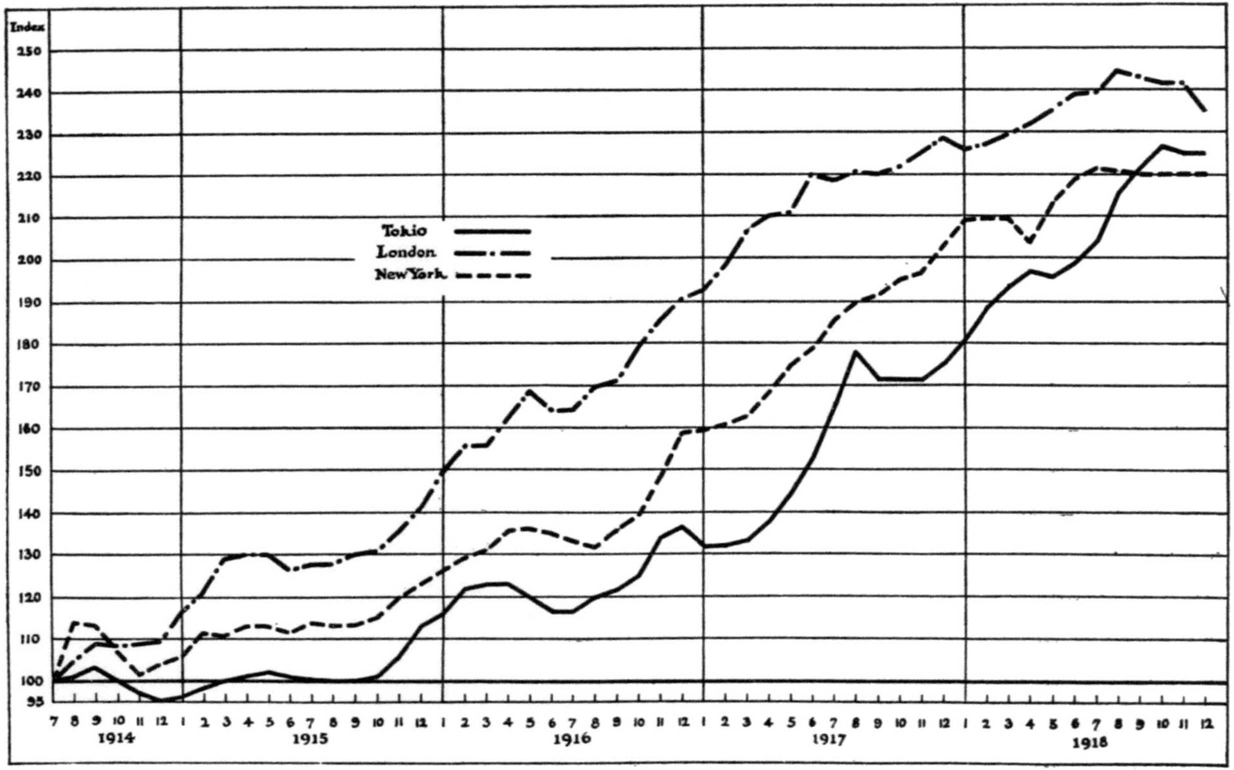

CHART I. TOKIO, LONDON AND NEW YORK WHOLESALE PRICES DURING THE WAR

(July 1914 = 100)

(Source: Bank of Japan, Economic Statistics of Japan, Tokio, 1925)

exchanges, for exchanges were kept as low as possible. The phenomena were just the reverse of those before the war. The condition of relatively high prices abroad is here shown by the accompanying Chart I, in which Tokio, London, and New York wholesale prices are compared.[1] Equally important are prces in Oriental countries. Prices in the Oriental countries also went up because of the temporary check of supply of European goods. Japan now saw her chance. After having overthrown the German naval base at Kiaochau and the South Seas in the early part of November 1914, she now could command the whole Oriental market and the over-seas shipping.

In ordinary years, it is characteristic of Japanese trade to have an excess of imports in the first half of the year and an excess of exports in the latter half of the year. But the increase of exports was so tremendous that this characteristic soon disappeared. The course of Japan's increase of commodity trade, especially that of exports, is suggested by the following table.

PER CENT OF INCREASE OR DECREASE (–) OF JAPAN'S TRADE COMPARED WITH 1913[2]

	Imports	*Exports*	*Total Trade*
1914	–18	–6	–13
1915	–27	12	–9
1916	4	78	38
1917	42	154	94
1918	129	210	167
1919	198	232	215

[1] *Cf.* Mitchell, Wesley C., *International Price Comparison during the War*, Government Printing Office, Washington, 1919, p. 34.

[2] This table is taken from the U. S. Tariff Commission's *The Foreign Trade of Japan*, Washington, 1922, p. 19. This table, however, is not based on figures which include the foreign trades of Chosen and Taiwan. If they had used the other figures and had corrected exports, the increase would have been still greater.

It is also interesting to note that Japan's trade profits of 1,566 million yen during the war-period were derived one-half from Asia and one-half from Europe and America combined. It is also noteworthy that Japan imported a great deal of raw materials and foodstuffs from Oriental countries, especially cotton and wool from India and Australia respectively.

Japan's Commodity Trade according to Countries during the War [1]

(million yen)

Asia	*Total exports of 5 years to*	*Total imports of 5 years from*	*Excess of imports (-) or exports*
China	1,435	912	521
Hongkong	214	2	207
India	442	977	-533
Asiatic Russia	319	12	303
Others	...	...	...
Total	2,761	2,260	499
Europe			
Great Britain	547	360	186
France	376	18	354
Italy	45	...	42
Russia	58	1	55
Others	...	...	...
Total	1,065	509	554
Others			
U. S. A.	1,748	1,387	359
Australia	146	165	-18

(B) Next is the invisible trade. Among the invisible trade items, most remarkable was the expansion of merchant marine and consequently the increase of freight receipts. With the increase of freights went also the increase of insurance premiums and charterage, the total of which was more than 1.353 million yen. The following figures may indicate the trend of their rapid growth.

[1] Figures are based on Department of Finance, *Kinyu Jikō*, 1924, pp. 224-227.

FREIGHT, INSURANCE AND CHARTERAGE RECEIPTS DURING THE WAR
(million yen)

	1914	*1915*	*1916*	*1917*	*1918*	*Total*
Freight	43	59	162	294	441	1,001
Insurance Premiums	6	14	21	43	110	195
Charterage	2	2	39	61	53	157
Total	49	75	222	398	604	1,353

Besides these, we must also note our receipts of immigrant remittances which amounted during the course of five years to 364 million yen, profits and interest of our foreign investments which amounted to 106 million yen, expenditures by foreign steamship companies in Japan which amounted to 52 million yen, the proceeds of sales of munitions which amounted to 337 million yen, and other governmental receipts which amounted to 76 million yen.

Against these receipts we had paid interests on foreign loans, premiums on insurance, profits and dividends payable to foreigners, expenditures of our steamship companies abroad, and expenditures of our nationals abroad. If we take all these together, we get the following balances for each year, making the total net receipt of 1,333 million yen.

We have seen that our total net balance of commodity trade was 1,292 million yen and our total net balance of invisible trade was 1,333 million yen, making a total net profit of 2,625 million yen for Japan during the War.[1] This was a clear profit. Although the sum cannot be compared with a huge excess of American exports during the period, namely, $11,800,000,000, yet it was the greatest profit Japan had

[1] Mr. J. Inoue's figure for Japan's net earning during the period is 2,800 million yen. But in his trade account, neither specie movements are included, nor trade figures are corrected. If he takes account of these, his figure may coincide with mine. J. Inoue, *Japan's Economic and Financial Situations after the War*, Tokio, 1925, p. 10, *passim*.

JAPAN'S INVISIBLE TRADE DURING THE WAR[1]
(million yen)

Receipts	*1914*	*1915*	*1916*	*1917*	*1918*	*Total*
I. Governmental:						
1. Sales of munitions, etc.	18.7	71.5	101.6	80.5	63.6	337.9
II. Private:						
1. Freight and charterage	43.3	61.9	175.8	294.9	495.1	1071.0
2. Expenditures of foreign ships and companies in Japan	11.8	8.0	9.5	12.7	10.8	52.8
3. Expenditures of foreigners in Japan	16.0	19.0	27.6	35.7	37.3	135.6
4. Profits by Japanese abroad, immigrants' remittance and those carried home	45.3	46.4	68.5	89.9	114.8	364.9
5. Profits and interest on foreign investments ..	2.8	3.0	18.5	36.7	45.8	106.8
6. Insurance & premiums	6.3	14.1	21.1	44.0	110.1	195.6
7. Others			18.4	40.4	17.8	76.6
Total	144.2	223.9	441.0	634.8	895.3	2339.2
Payments						
I. Governmental:						
1. Interest	63.1	64.0	52.3	52.4	50.2	282.0
2. Other payments	15.4	15.3	17.8	20.4	52.5	121.4
Total	78.5	79.3	70.1	72.8	102.7	403.4
II. Private:						
1. Expenditures of our ships abroad	16.1	20.3	27.4	33.8	50.8	148.4
2. Expenditures of Japanese abroad	9.2	7.9	10.4	14.1	22.6	64.2
3. Profits by foreigners in Japan	8.7	7.4	7.7	9.7	11.1	44.6
4. Interest and profits of foreign investments ..	25.5	22.4	22.4	23.5	23.7	117.2
5. Insurance & premiums	7.1	14.2	18.9	60.4	98.1	198.7
6. Expenditures of Japanese enterprises abroad	5.7	3.1	.9	3.1	3.1	15.9
7. Others	.2	.2	6.2	1.9	5.2	13.7
Total	150.7	154.8	164.0	219.3	317.3	1006.1
Net Balance	–6.5	69.1	277.0	415.5	578.0	1333.1

These figures which exclude bonds, debentures and other capital movements are compiled from J. Inoue's *Japan's International Finance at Present and her Financial Policy* (*Waga-kokusai Kinyuno Genjho oyobi Zengosaku*), Tokio, 1926, Appendix vii. Unfortunately there had been no government figures of this kind. Mr. J. Inoue was once the governor of the Bank of Japan, of the Yokohama Specie Bank, and was at one time Finance Minister. So the above figures are the most dependable of their kind under the circumstances.

ever made. To restate the rapid growth of Japan's net earning, we have the following:

RAPID GROWTH OF JAPAN'S NET EARNING DURING THE WAR
(million yen)

	1914	*1915*	*1916*	*1917*	*1918*	*Total*
Net balance of visible trade	22	211	345	380	334	1,292
Net balance of invisible trade	-6	69	277	415	578	1,333
Net earning	16	280	622	795	912	2,625

(C) The earning of this huge sum was, of course, possible because of the great European War. But somehow Japan was potentially capable to meet this great emergency and to turn the whole tide to her profit. For our immediate study, however, it is significant to note that a debtor country in 1913 with 1,969 million yen could now not only pay all the debts owed, but also leave with her still 656 million yen. This financial transformation is most significant. Its effect on yen exchange is easily traceable. But before we come to that, let us see a little more clearly how this financial change took place. First let us note how this 2,625 million yen credit was distributed among her debit accounts. The biggest channel into which this credit went was the subscription to foreign loans and treasury notes in Japan. Beginning with February, 1916 to the end of the war, Russia, England, France and Italy borrowed from Japan to the aggregate sum of 700 million yen. She also bought foreign bonds to the amount of 247 million yen within the period, making a total of 947 million yen debit to these foreign countries. The next biggest item in the debit account was her accumulation of gold abroad. The net increase of gold funds abroad in five years was more than 890 million yen. Likewise, the exchange funds held by the Japanese branch banks abroad was increased in five years by 523 million yen.[1] Last of all, we redeemed our bonds abroad

[1] This figure was arrived at by a deductive method after having in-

and bought back our domestic bonds which went out before the war, all of which amounted to 265 million yen for the period. If we add all these together, we get 2,625 million yen on the debit side, which exactly balances the enormous credit as we have already seen.

To be a little more detailed, we have each year decreased our foreign bonds held abroad, and greatly increased our foreign investments together with our exchange funds, as will be seen herewith.

NET CAPITAL MOVEMENT DURING THE WAR [1]

(million yen)

	1914	1915	1916	1917	1918	Total
Credit:						
1. Foreign investments in Japan [2]	9	......	......	......	......	......
2. Net decrease of gold funds abroad	31	......	......	......	......	......
Total	40	......	......	......	......	40
Debit:						
1. Realizing of investments by foreigners [2]	......	42	125	55	50	......
2. Japanese investments abroad [3]	......	35	371	283	258	......
3. Net increase of gold funds held abroad	......	167	107	158	491	......
4. Net increase of bankers' exchange funds abroad [4]	56	36	19	299	113	......
Total	......	......	......	......	......	2,665
Net Balance	16	280	622	795	912	2,625

vestigated all other figures. The figure, however, roughly corresponds to the one arrived at by K. Maeda who was once Secretary to the president of Yokohama Specie Bank. *Vide*, K. Maeda, *A Study of Yen Exchange*, Tokio, 1925, p. 70.

[1] The official reports of this kind are completely lacking in Japan. This is a rough approximation, the best the writer could make with the present available sources.

[2] These figures were arrived at by comparing the outstanding amounts

Thus, if we recapitulate what has been said of Japan's international economic situation during 1914 to 1918, we get the following summary statement:

of national foreign bonds, domestic bonds sold out, prefectural bonds sold out, debentures sold out, and estimates of increase or decrease of foreigners' capital in Japan. These detailed figures can be seen in Department of Finance, *Kinyu Jikō Sankosho*, Tokio, 1924, p. 26. This may be further illustrated by the increase or decrease of foreign investments in Japan as follows:

OUTSTANDING AMOUNTS OF FOREIGN INVESTMENTS IN JAPAN, 1914-1918
(million yen)

At the end of	Gov't Foreign Bonds (floated abroad)	Domestic Bonds sold out	Local Gov't Bonds	Debentures (floated abroad)	Foreigners' Invest-ment in Japan	Total	Increase or de-crease (—)
1913....	1,524	74	177	166	26	1,969	115
1914....	1,524	81	177	166	29	1,978	9
1915 ...	1,493	71	176	166	28	1,936	—42
1916....	1,384	56	175	166	26	1,809	—127
1917....	1,348	40	172	166	26	1,754	—54
1918....	1,311	31	168	165	27	1,704	—50

[3] These figures were arrived at by supplementing the *Kinyu Jikō Sankosho*, *ibid.*, p. 41 with figures of the Kokumin Shimbun, Dec. 26, 1926 "Taishono Seidaini okeru Kokuryoku Shincho," *cf.* K. Maeda's *ibid.*, pp. 71-72. Of these 700 million yen were subscribed for the Russian Treasury notes, England's exchequer bonds, France and Italy's Treasury notes. The famous Nishihara loans for China were made during this period. *Cf.* Dr. C. F. Remer, *The Foreign Trade of China*, Shanghai, 1926, p. 226. The other 247 million yen were variously invested, such as buying foreign bonds, actually investing in China and the South Seas.

[4] The official reports of this kind are completely lacking in Japan. This is a rough approximation, the best the writer could make with the present available sources.

BALANCE OF INTERNATIONAL PAYMENTS, 1914-1918
(millions of yen)

Credits	1914	1915	1916	1917	1918	Total
Exports of merchandise (net)	2	191	417	618	338	
Exports of gold and silver	20	20	...	...	...	
Freight and other invisibile receipts (net)	..	69	277	415	578	
Foreign debts	7	...	...	...	...	
Realizing Japanese investments abroad	33	...	...	...	...	
Total credits	62	280	694	1,033	916	2,985
Debits						
Imports of gold and silver	..	...	72	238	4	
Invisible net payments	6	...	...	...	...	
Realizing of investments by foreigners	..	42	125	55	50	
Japanese investments abroad	..	35	371	283	358	
Increase of gold funds held abroad	..	167	107	158	491	
Bankers exchange funds, unreported funds, etc.[1]	56	38	19	299	113	
Total debits	62	280	694	1,033	916	2,985

(D) Before the War and up to 1916, London was the center of all exchanges. That is to say, practically all of the business of the world was cleared through London. Business men, bankers and international financiers "have discovered from experience that their bill, drawn against a bank in London, has offered the most convenient and the cheapest method of discharging the collection and financing functions required to complete international mercantile transactions." [2] The Japanese are no exception in availing themselves of the facilities furnished by London. To illustrate: our export bills, whether they were drawn against Chinese or Indian importers of our textile fabrics or drawn against American

[1] For detail, see the above table of net capital movement.

[2] Edgar S. Furniss, *Foreign Exchange, the Financial Mechanism of International Commerce*, Boston, 1922, p. 313.

importers of our raw silk, were alike made payable at London. Likewise, our importers were willing to pay for their import goods in sterling bills drawn against them payable, for instance, at a demand rate of exchange on London. So the Japanese bankers naturally have carried large exchange funds in London. Consequently, our foreign exchange rates, whether rates on silver China or gold America, were based primarily on Japan-London exchange. For instance, a rate of exchange on New York in Japan was primarily based on the rate of exchange on London and adjusted by a current rate of New York-London exchange. This can easily be seen, for what they were after was not to get so many dollars or rupees, but to get as many pounds sterling as possible.

But with the breakdown of London as the center of exchanges and as a free gold market, and with the ascendancy of New York, such a practice of basing all other exchanges on London exchange became no longer profitable. New York began to offer better exchange facilities. So they began, after 1916, to keep more exchange funds in New York than in London. The consequence was that they now began to base all other exchanges upon New York-London cross-rates, as their interests were now shifted to the dollars rather than to English pounds. Thus the shifting of the financial center from London to New York caused a fundamental change in the workings of exchange operation in Japan.

Still another change took place during the course of the war, for on September 7, 1917 when America established a gold embargo, Japan could no longer remove the exchange funds created in New York to pay her imports, for instance, from India. And India was not importing to any great amount from the United States to effect a triangular exchange. On the other hand, Japan's excess of exports was piling up more and more exchange funds in New York.

Exchange was fast becoming one-sided, and the yen was rising higher and higher, showing thereby that the difference in the balance of payments was a determining factor of exchange more than anything else and even more than the relative level of prices, for at this time Japan's level of prices was rising almost as high as America's.[1] Another effect of the American gold embargo on Japanese exchange was the initiation of the yen bill. The dollar domiciled bill,[2] which was just initiated by the establishment of the Federal Reserve system in America and the use of which was also favored by the Japanese in the Oriental trade, was now hampered by the American embargo. So the use of direct yen exchange bills was fostered by Japanese bankers. But while this was under way, the world war came to an end. Meanwhile, the government stepped in each time when exchange difficulties arose and tried to relieve the situation by adopting various exchange policies, the details of which will be discussed later.

With this general description of the change of Japanese exchange situation, let us now trace more fully the fluctuations of yen exchange in reference to Great Britain, France, Russia, United States, China and India and see what causal or other relations there were between prices and exchange or between exchange and balance of payments.

4. JAPANESE BRITISH EXCHANGE

Immediately before the War, as was explained previously, the Japanese-British exchange was always kept two or three points below par.[3] But when the War broke out the first

[1] *Vide* chart I, *supra*, p. 59. Tokio prices went even higher than New York prices after September, 1918.

[2] By the dollar domiciled bill is meant such indirect exchange bills like Kobe payable New York, Yokohama Payable New York, Shanghai payable New York, etc.

[3] The par is *S*2/0-9/16. One point is 1/16 of one penny.

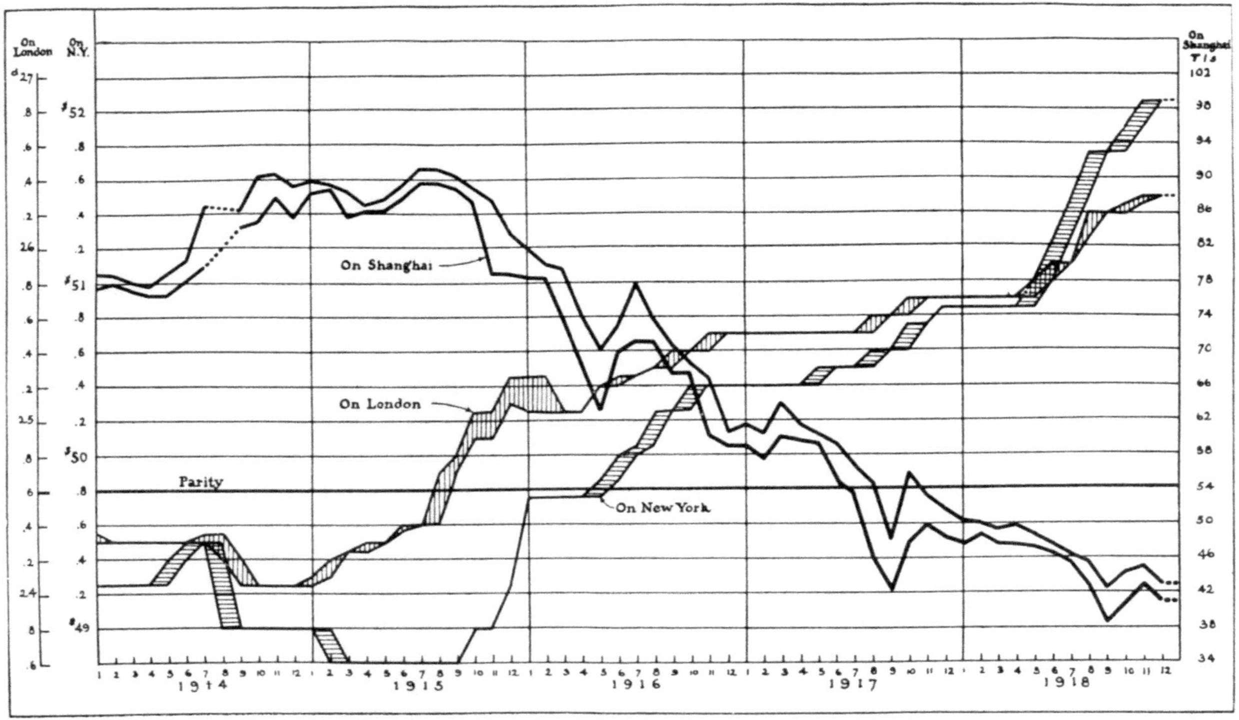

Chart II. Exchanges on London, New York and Shanghai during the War
(Monthly high and low T. T. Rates)
Par on London *d.* 24.576 per Y 1.00
Par on New York $49.85 per Y 100.00
(Source: Yokohama Specie Bank's Weekly)

week of August, 1914, all exchanges in Japan came to a standstill until the 13th of the same month, and after August 15, export bills were slowly reintroduced, and by September exchanges became fairly settled on the former basis. But the amount of bills on London was gradually diminished as time went on, for such bills, like silk export bills, began to go to New York direct instead of London. During the next year, 1915, sterling in Japan fell in value an average of 3 per cent below par, and 4½ per cent in 1916, 5 per cent in 1917 and 8 per cent in 1918. The trend of this gradual fall may be seen by the upward trend of the yen exchange on London in the accompanying Chart II.[1] Such a fall of the British pound was not only evidenced in the Japanese-British exchange, but also in all other exchanges where British money was involved. For instance, in the New York-London exchange, the most dominant and perhaps the standard exchange of the world, we see that the value of the pound gradually fell. In 1915 it fell an average of 2 per cent; in 1916, 1917 and 1918 it fell 3 per cent below par.[2] This general fall of British exchange may be attributed (1) to a great rise of prices [3] accompanied by a great excess of imports, (2) to a curtailment of production, (3) to a great decrease in non-trade receipts, caused mainly by her merchant marine, as it was obliged to be engaged in non-trade business. But the fall was much relieved by pegging. If it were not pegged it would have fallen much more severely and at an earlier date. Pegging was accomplished by the

[1] Remember, however, these are pegged rates of the Yokohama Specie Bank. The actual exchanges were much higher than these curves. Yet notice the wide spreads of the exchanges.

[2] Federal Reserve *Bulletin*, November, 1920, p. 1159.

[3] *See* Chart I, *supra*, p. 59. This great rise was mainly caused by inflation of currency. *See* Table D, p. 99, Paper No. 111, Brussels International Financial Conference; also T. E. Gregory, *Foreign Exchange*, London, 1922, p. 114.

British government by (1) her shipments of specie, (2) return of American securities, (3) sales of foreign securities in New York, (4) loans by the United States, and (5) trade restrictions over unnecessary imports. Before the American entrance of the war,[1] Great Britain arranged for the stabilization of the pound with private bankers—chiefly with J. P. Morgan and Co.—in the United States, and after the American entrance, she received loans direct from the American government.[2] Thus the exchange was practically pegged at $4.76½ throughout the rest of the war.

Such were the general causes which predominantly were responsible in fixing the value of the British pound. And to these general causes, the Japanese-British situation contributed a part, for Japan's foreign exchange with England, though small in amount from the British standpoint, was carried on first through London and later through New York. The triangular operation among these three corners became much more common, whereas with other countries direct exchanges were more favored as the result of disturbed exchange conditions.

I have already referred to the relatively higher level of prices in England and relatively lower prices in Japan. And these, coupled with the military needs, effected a heavy importation of Japanese goods into England, and turned the whole tide of what was formerly characterized as Japan's over-imports of English goods to that of England's over-imports of Japanese goods. The following statistics will vindicate this statement:

[1] U. S. A. entered into the War on April 24, 1917.

[2] A somewhat similar summary was reached by Ruth M. Jaeger, *Stabilizing of the Foreign Exchanges*, Columbia, 1924, p. 21; and Ira B. Cross, *Domestic and Foreign Exchange*, New York, 1923, pp. 536-7; U. S. Senate Commission on Gold and Silver Inquiry, *Foreign Currency and Exchange Investigation*, series 9, Washington, 1925, vol. i, pp. 290-6; vol. ii, pp. 290-292 (editor, J. P. Young).

JAPANESE ENGLISH TRADE DURING THE WAR[1]

(million yen)

	Exports to England	Imports from England	Excess of trade
1902	17	50	-33
1907	22	116	-93
1912	29	116	-86
1913	32	122	-89
1914	33	92	59
1915	68	58	10
1916	102	81	20
1917	202	63	139
1918	142	66	76

And for this excess of exports of Japan, England began to offset by borrowing in Japan. Such and other borrowings which began after 1916 amounted at one time to more than 742 million yen, while Japan's net payment to England other than trade was becoming nil. Thus the statistical analysis shows that in the Japan-England relationship, prices in England first went up, followed by great over-imports. As Japan's excess of exports to England increased, its exchange on London gradually rose (or the value of sterling gradually fell). In other words, the *steady* rise of Japanese-British exchange was largely caused by the balance of payment,[2] although much was done by pegging as in other British exchanges.

5. JAPANESE-FRENCH EXCHANGE

What has been said with regard to England also holds true of France. According to the statistics prepared by the Brussels International Conference, French prices and note issues were as follows:

[1] Department of Finance, *Kinyu Jikō Sankosho*, 1924, Tokio, p. 223.

[2] *See* Chart II, on p. 69, and compare London exchange and the balance of payments.

PRICES DURING THE WAR [1]

(1913 – 100)

	1914	*1915*	*1916*	*1917*	*1918*
France	116	169	206	309	358
Japan	91	108	131	166	214

NOTE ISSUES DURING THE WAR

(1913 – 100)

	1914	*1915*	*1916*	*1917*	*1918*
France	117	233	292	391	530
Japan	90	101	141	195	256

Under such favorable conditions, Japan's excess of exports to France was remarkable.

JAPANESE–FRENCH TRADE DURING THE WAR [2]

(million yen)

	Exports to France	*Imports from France*	*Excess of Exports*
1914	31	4	26
1915	42	3	38
1916	64	4	59
1917	97	4	93
1918	142	3	138

France's trade was unfavorable not only with Japan but also with all other countries. Her total excess of imports during the War was more than 62 billion francs,[3] against which she had never more than 3 billion francs in her net non-trade receipts. Hence France began to ship gold, neutral stocks and bonds, and French treasury bills.[4] In

[1] Brussels International Financial Conference, Table C, page 99, Paper No. 111. According to U. S. Federal Reserve *Bulletin*, statistics are about same. (Federal Reserve *Bulletin*, Dec., 1921, p. 1463.)

	1913	*1914*	*1915*	*1916*	*1917*	*1918*
France	100	101	137	187	262	339
Japan	100	96	97	117	147	192

[2] Department of Finance, *Kinyu Jikō*, 1924, p. 223.

[3] The figure is based on the *Statesman's Year-Book*, 1918, p. 831; 1920, p. 846; and U. S. Senate Commission, *ibid.*, p. 483.

[4] France exported 1,955 million francs in gold to the Bank of England

other countries, too, France attempted to borrow funds by using neutral securities as collateral. By the end of December, 1917, the Bank of France reported that the total securities mobilized amounted to 640 million francs. And after the American entrance into the war, she borrowed from America more than three billion dollars.[1] Such an unprecedented unfavorable balance of payments had expressed itself in her exchange rates. The franc, for instance, was kept slightly below par in New York before February, 1915, but after March it gradually went down as the French current debits increased. In 1916 the average discount was more than 12 per cent, although this percentage was reduced to 9 per cent when America began to finance her.[2]

This general trend of French exchange was well reflected in the Japanese-French exchange. The par between France and Japan is fr. 2.5833. At the end of 1915 the franc

and over 20 billion francs of treasury bills to England, to stabilize the franc, before the American entrance of the War. *See* Ruth M. Jaeger, *Stabilization of the Foreign Exchanges*, Columbia, 1924, p. 33.

[1] *The Statesman's Year Book*, 1920, p. 838. According to Professor Charles Gide, France financed the War only 16 per cent by taxation and the rest by loans, domestic and foreign. Foreign loans were 27 milliard francs, constituting 17 per cent of the total war expenses. Of these 27 milliards francs, much was used for exchange pegging. His figures are as follows. (Charles Gide, "French War Budgets for 1919-1920," *Economic Journal*, June 1919, p. 132.)

French War Expenses, Aug. 1, 1914 to April 1, 1919
(milliard francs)

22	by taxation	16	per cent
54	by loan in the form of "rentes perpetuelles"	33	"
32	by short term bonds	20	"
26	by loans from the Bank of France (in the form of note issue)	14	"
27	by foreign loans (chiefly from England and U. S. A.)	17	"
161		100	

[2] *See* Federal Reserve *Bulletin*, November 1920, p. 1159.

went as high as fr. 2.93 or its value went down 13 per cent. During 1916 and 1917, the franc was at an average discount of 22 per cent, and although in July 1918 it went as high as fr. 3.20, the French exchange remained around 20 per cent discount during the rest of the war period in Japan. The fall was, therefore, first due to her unbalanced payments caused by her high prices and war needs, and then aided by speculation. But, again, as in the case of England, the fall was much checked by *pegging* through international borrowing.

6. JAPANESE-RUSSIAN EXCHANGE

The fall of the value of the Russian ruble in Japan was as serious as in other countries. The following may be compared.[1]

AVERAGE EXCHANGE RATES ON RUSSIA

	At Yokohama on Harbin[2]	*At New York on Petrograd*
	Y 100 = R. 96.87	R 1. = 51.46 c
July, 1914........	R. 102.10	51.28
Dec. "	120.50	42.00
April, 1915	119.00	43.12
Aug. "	140.00	34.00
Dec. "	175.00	31.25
April, 1916........	169.00	31.00
Aug. "	170.00	32.07
Dec. "	179.00	29.77
April, 1917........	183.00	28.52
Aug. "	295.00	19.35
Dec. "	400.00	13.00
April, 1918........	360.00	14.00
Aug. "	590.00	14.00
Dec. "	520.00	14.00

[1] Yokohama-Harbin exchanges are based on the Yokohama Specie Bank's reports, while New-York-Petrograd's are based on *Harvard Review of Economic Statistics*, July, 1919.

[2] Harbin is a Chinese City in North Manchuria but with Russian monetary influence. In Asiatic Russia Harbin is generally chosen with Vladvostock as two Russian exchange centres.

From the above, one will see that the Russian ruble depreciated in value rapidly until December, 1917 when its nominal value became almost one-fourth of its former value. The chief cause before the Revolution of March, 1917, undoubtedly, was inflation. At the time of the Revolution the total note issue was more than 11 times the amount before the War.[1] On the other hand, Russia was borrowing very heavily from England, France, the United States and Japan. These loans amounted to 5,500 million rubles in all. Japan alone loaned her 200 million yen to defray the excess of our exports consisting chiefly of munitions which amounted to 350 million yen.

But the more sensational fall beginning October, 1917 was largely due to speculation because of the Bolshevik Revolution in November, 1917, to her repudiation in January, 1918 of all foreign debts and interest incurred by preceding governments and a great currency inflation.

Before the War Y. 100 could purchase 96.87 rubles, but now—in October 1917—the same Y. 100 could buy more than 400 rubles. The introduction of the "NEP" in 1921 was still helpless in restoring her rapidly falling exchanges. It was only after November, 1922, when the gold chervonetz (notes) (1 chervonetz = 10 rubles gold) was introduced that the Russian exchange became fairly stabilized.[2] But at any rate, the Russian exchange after the Revolution was of little practical value, because there had been practically no trade with Soviet Russia until quite recently.[3] Thus the strength of the Japanese yen increased first as her balance of payments to Russia increased and then by speculation as the Russian credit became doubtful and risky.

[1] U. S. Senate Commission, *Foreign Currency and Exchange Investigation*, Washington, 1925, vol. ii, p. 190.

[2] U. S. Senate Commission, *ibid.*, pp. 198-220.

[3] Savel Zimand, *State Capitalism in Russia, New York*, 1927, pp. 21-23.

7. JAPANESE-AMERICAN EXCHANGE

As the War prolonged, the Allied countries began to rely more upon American goods and American finance. And America amply supplied both. During the course of five years, the United States had exported an excess of more than 11 billion dollars worth of goods.[1] Of this sum, only about one billion dollars was paid for in gold,[2] and the rest had to be settled by the use of credit. About 2 billion dollars worth of American securities were bought back, and about 8 billion dollars were paid for by the new American loans to the Allied countries during the War.[3]

Coupled with this favorable trade balance and large foreign investments, the discount market of New York wonderfully developed especially after the creation of the Federal Reserve Banking system in November, 1914. America was somewhat like Japan. During the war her gold standard was least impaired. Consequently after 1916, New York became the center of world finance and has become the clear-

[1] According to *Harvard Review of Economic Statistics*, 1919, p. 235, figures are as follows:

AMERICAN FOREIGN TRADE DURING THE WAR
(million dollars)

	Exports	*Imports*	*Excess of Exports*
1914	2,113	1,789	324
1915	3,554	1,778	1,776
1916	5,482	2,391	3,091
1917	6,233	2,552	3,281
1918	6,149	3,031	3,117
			11,600

[2] John H. Williams, Foreign Exchange, "Prices and the Course of International Trade," *The Annals of American Academy of Political and Social Science*, May, 1920, p. 198.

[3] George W. Edwards, *Investing in Foreign Securities*, New York, 1926, p. 58.

ing house of international payments. The world's exchanges were now centered around New York.

The Japanese yen exchange before 1916, as already mentioned, was primarily based on the value of the British pound, for it was through the British money we made our foreign payments and receipts. But with the ascendancy of New York, Japanese bankers began to keep larger funds in New York to settle not only trade accounts with America but also trade accounts with India, China, Australia, Europe, etc. One natural result of this change was that the Japanese exchange now had to be based upon the value of the dollar instead of the pound sterling, for it was now through the dollar that we settled our foreign accounts. Formerly, a fall of New York-London exchange, for instance, was thought of in Japan as a rise in the value of the dollar and not a fall of the English money, for then £1 was still £1 to the Japanese. And so Japanese bankers, whenever such a fall occurred, tried to reduce their rates on New York accordingly. This is why we have seen a rather abnormal fall of yen exchange on New York during 1915[1] when the London exchange in New York fell.[2] But after 1916, when Japanese bankers began to keep more funds in New York, even a slight up or down of the dollar exchange became a matter of direct interest to Japan. In other words, to the Japanese business man, too, the dollar exchange has now come to be the standard exchange with which they have to deal in foreign trade.

We have already seen that Japanese prices were relatively lower than American prices during the War, although toward the end of the period, Japanese prices went slightly higher than American prices.[3] This had a very good

[1] *See* Chart II on p. 69.

[2] *See* Federal Reserve *Bulletin*, November, 1920, p. 1159.

[3] *See* Chart I on p. 59.

effect on Japan's exports to America. In five years she earned net exports amounting to 413 million yen, for which she received 333 million yen net in gold, leaving a surplus of 80 milion yen credit, the details of which are herewith given.

JAPAN'S TRADE WITH U. S. A. DURING THE WAR

(million yen)

	Exports	*Imports*	*Excess*	*4% technical correction*	*Total excess of exports*
1914	196	96	99	3	102
1915	204	102	101	4	105
1916	340	204	136	8	144
1917	478	359	118	14	132
1918	530	628	-95	25	-70
					413

GOLD MOVEMENT WITH U. S. A.

(million yen)

	Exports	*Imports*	*Excess of exports*
1914	16	..	16
1915	39	..	39
1916	..	50	-50
1917	..	338	-338
1918	..	..	..
			-333

Besides these trade balances, Japan got from America immigrants' remittances, freight and insurance charges. Added to these were what England, France, and Italy owed us by their excess of imports of our goods, as these accounts also had to be cleared through New York.

So one can easily see that the balance of payments was now one-sided. And as the volume of such payments increased the yen exchange rose. Already in May, 1916, the exchange on New York was above par. During the rest of the year it still rose, and gold was imported to the amount of 50 million yen. The next year, 1917, saw even larger shipments of gold amounting to 338 million yen.[1] Thus by specie flow America kept the value of yen down around $51⅞ even after she went into the War in April, 1917. But no sooner was this limit broken than America put a ban on gold exports in September of the same year. The exchange went up to $52⅛ in December; and in June, 1918 it went up to $53⅛; in November, $54.00; and in December, $54⅝ or almost 10 per cent premium.

The Japanese-American exchange might have risen more if the Japanese government had not stepped in to try to relieve the situation. The rising of Japanese-American exchange was detrimental to Japanese exporters, while it was the source of constant worry for the Japanese bankers, for they hated to see funds in New York depreciate in terms of yen. Such dollar funds were at one time considered to have exceeded $250,000,000. The Japanese government was, therefore, buying these funds heavily from exchange bankers at lower rates of exchange, and thereby advancing them with more Bank and Treasury notes. For this reason the Yokohama Specie Bank had to maintain artificially lower rates of exchange than the ordinary market rates, differences being sometimes as great as $3.75. For instance, the following may be compared:

Demand Rates on New York in 1918[2]

	August	*Sept.*	*Oct.*
Yokohama Specie Bank	$51.⅞	51.⅞	52.00
Foreign Branch Banks	$54.⅛	54.⅜	54.½
Difference	$ 3.¾	3.½	2.½

[1] Department of Finance, *Kinyu Jikō*, 1924, p. 235. *See* also Federal Reserve *Bulletin*, Aug., 1919, p. 731.

[2] *Cf.* K. Maeda, *Study of Yen Exchange*, Tokio, 1925, p. 117. Moreover, between New York market and Yokohama Specie Bank, there were following differences in 1918. Although these differences were smaller

As a result of such differences, all export bills were assembled at the Yokohama Specie Bank, and all import bills came to the foreign branch banks. Because by so doing Japanese exporters could get more money for their export bills, and importers needed to pay less money for their import goods. And the foreign branch bankers were financing evenly between export and import bills, whereas the Japanese bankers headed by the Yokohama Specie Bank were financing one-sidedly and thereby accumulating more and more funds in New York, a tendency which they did not like but which under the circumstances could not be helped. At any rate, the exchange was thus pegged at little below par during 1914 to May, 1916 and at a little above par for the next year, and still at higher levels for the next ten months and at greatly higher levels for the rest of the period, the highest being a 10 per cent premium, as already mentioned. It is also noteworthy that, although after September, 1918, Japanese prices became relatively higher than American prices, yet the

than those in Japan, it clearly indicates the amounts of pegging done by the Japanese government.

Month	*Yokohama Specie Bank's D. D. on New York* * (*high*)	*New York Exchange on Yokohama D. D.*† (*high*)	*Difference*
1918 1	51	51.875	.875
2	51	51.65	.65
3	51	51.75	.75
4	51	51.90	.90
5	51.125	52.75	1.625
6	51.375	52.90	1.525
7	51.625	53.75	2.125
8	51.875	54.63	2.755
9	51.875	54.63	2.755
10	52.	54.75	2.75
11	52.25	54.75	2.5
12	52.25	53.25	2.5

* According to the official rates of the Yokohama Specie Bank.

† Federal Reserve *Bulletin*, April, 1922, p. 488.

greater depreciation of the dollar relatively to the yen took place in these four months,[1] showing clearly that the raised American exchange rates were the result of uneven balance of payments and the American gold embargo. But the one underlying dominant force during this period was the trend of a relatively lower level of prices in Japan, giving occasion for more exports not only to America directly but also to all other countries where money was paid through New York, thus resulting in a one-sided balance of payments in favor of Japan.

8. JAPANESE-CHINESE EXCHANGE

Hitherto we have seen that the Japanese exchange was largely determined and affected by Japan's favorable balance of payments due to relatively higher prices abroad and war needs. Exchange was hardly a cause of either high prices or balance of trade for any great length of period. But with China the case was different. The exchange on China had influenced the Japanese-Chinese trade much more than the trade could influence the exchange. In dealing with the Chinese exchange, no one can deny that the predominant factor was the price of silver. So let us note the relative import-

[1] Statistical Bureau of the Bank of Japan shows their index number as follows. (Bank of Japan, *Economic Statistics of Japan*, 1925).

Year	*Month*	*Tokio Index number*	*New York Index number*	*Exchange on New York* *	*Exchange on Japan at New York* †
1914	7	100	100	$49.50	$49.90
1918	8	216	221	51.75	54.60
	9	222	220	51.75	54.63
	10	227	220	51.87	54.75
	11	225	220	52.12	54.75
	12	225	220	52.12	53.25

* Yokohama Specie Bank's T. T. rates.

† Federal Reserve *Bulletin*, April, 1922, p. 488. D. D. rates on Yokohama.

ance of these factors as revealed in the Japanese-Chinese exchange.

First of all, the balance of payments with China was not greatly one-sided. The characteristic of Japanese-Chinese trade before the War was our excess of exports, by 60 to 90 million yen per year in exchange for our manufactured goods for Chinese raw materials. This characteristic remained throughout the war, although during this period our imports from China increased 415 per cent while our exports to China increased only by 258 per cent. The silver movement was insignificant in amount, and gold was shipped in 1916 and 1917, mainly to South Manchuria, Shanghai and other places where gold was needed to facilitate the Japanese trade and to stabilize the value of the yen. The figures may be seen below.

JAPAN'S TRADE WITH CHINA DURING THE WAR [1]

(million yen)

	Exports	*Imports*	*Excess of Exports*	*Total*
1913	184	92	92	
1914	184	89	95	
1915	163	113	49	
1916	229	142	87	521
1917	384	186	197	
1918	475	382	93	

GOLD AND SILVER MOVEMENT WITH CHINA

(million yen)

	Exports		*Imports*		*Excess*		
	Gold	*Silver*	*Gold*	*Silver*	*Gold*	*Silver*	*Total*
1914	1	1	7	1	-5	-	-5
1915	-	2	7	-	-6	2	-4
1916	16	3	1	-	14	3	17
1917	24	-	1	4	23	-3	20
1918	—	-	-	2	—	-2	-2

Most of these trade credits, together with freightage, insurance charges, etc., were invested in Chinese industries in

[1] Department of Finance, *Kinyu Jiko*, 1924, pp. 222-240.

Shanghai, Tientsin, and elsewhere; while some of these credits went out to India and other Oriental countries in the form of silver.

And as the years went on, the balance of payments was increasing in favor of Japan, yet the tael was rising in value, a phenomenon which does not agree with the theory of balance of payments; but it agrees with the price of silver. For silver had fluctuated the same way as did the tael, while trade was much influenced by the fall or rise of silver and, therefore, by exchange rates. The following statistics may be compared.

PRICES OF SILVER AND THE TAEL DURING THE WAR [1]

Silver per 1 troy ounce in New York

		c		c		c
1914	high	59.250	low	47.625	average	54.6875
1915		56.500		46.750		49.6875
1916		76.625		55.875		65.5000
1917		108.500		71.750		81.3750
1918		101.125		85.925		96.7500

Exchange on Shanghai per y 100.00

		Tls		*Tls*		*Tls*
1914	high	90.50	low	76.50	average	81.873
1915		91.25		79.00		87.822
1916		82.00		60.25		71.025
1917		64.00		42.25		55.199
1918		50.25		38.50		45.741

As the price of silver rose, so also rose the value of the tael. For instance, when the average price of silver in 1914 was 54 cents per ounce we could get an average of 81.873 taels for every Y. 100. But in 1918 when the price of silver went up to 96 cents, or nearly doubled, the price we could get was only 45.741 taels or almost one-half the former amount. This rise in the value of the tael was continuous

[1] Department of Finance, *Kinyu Jikō*, 1924, p. 298.

throughout the war, and it is best seen by the corresponding fall of the yen against Shanghai in Chart II, page 69.

The reason why silver went high may be explained simultaneously from two sides; namely, the supply side and the demand side of silver. On the supply side, we find a decrease in the production of silver the chief cause.

World Production of Silver during the War [1]

(in million)

	Fine ounces	*Value*		*Fine ounces*	*Value*
1909	212	$110	1914	172	$ 95
1910	221	119	1915	173	89
1911	226	122	1916	180	124
1912	230	141	1917	186	166
1913	210	126	1918	203	200
Total	1,099	618	Total	914	674

From this, one will see that, although the commercial value of silver production in 1914-18 increased little over that of 1909-13, yet that was simply due to the higher price of silver during the war period, for in physical production the period preceding the War had produced almost twice as much silver as the war period. This decrease in the war period was largely due to the Mexican and Australian situations. Before the War, Mexico was the biggest silver-producing country of the world, producing 75 million ounces per year. But during the War, Mexico had constant internal trouble, which prevented her from producing more than half as much as she produced before the War. Likewise, Australia was producing before the War 14 to 18 million ounces. But owing to the war and high prices, many silver mines were closed, and only 4 million ounces were produced each year. The same thing was true of Canada and other countries with the single exception of the United

[1] These are estimates by the U. S. Bureau of the Mint as quoted in *The World Almanac for 1926*, New York, p. 268.

States. Even the United States reached its maximum production in 1914 with 75 million ounces, and was slowly decreasing its production after that date.[1]

On the other hand, demand for silver was persistent. The War created a need for more silver for coinage and reserve purposes. Various nations went into silver embargo.[2] Even the United States and Mexico went into the embargo in September, 1917, while the demand in India and China continued. In China, silver was demanded not only for domestic money circulation, but also as the only practical means to offset her excess of imports.

The increasing demand for silver and its decreasing supply was not only in harmony with the movement of the tael, thereby proving that there was a close correlation between the two and hindered trade, but also caused a wide fluctuation in the silver exchange itself, making a wide spread of 4, 5 taels in the course of a few days; speculation running wild, especially in Shanghai; and this again hindered trade greatly. But this does not mean that in China the metallist theory works. On the contrary, one must understand that in China the bulk of the means of payment is silver. Hence, the situation created by the relative amount of silver in China roughly corresponds to that created by the relative amount of bank notes in gold-standard countries. Therefore, the two are not contradictory in theory, but are in the same line of thought.

Thus in the case of Japanese-Chinese exchange much was attributable to the dearness of silver, which influenced the exchange, and this in turn influenced the balance of payments.

[1] *See* trends of silver production of various countries in the charts of Edwin R. A. Seligman, *Principles of Economics,* 11th ed., pp. 476-7.

[2] England in April 1918, France in August 1915, Australia in August 1914, Canada in August 1918, Mexico in September 1917, U. S. in September 1917, India in September 1917, and Japan in September 1917, went into silver embargo.

9. JAPANESE-INDIAN EXCHANGE

Another phase of silver exchange may be presented by the Japanese-Indian exchange. Although, theoretically speaking, exchange with India was based on the gold-exchange system, yet practically speaking, since the break-down of that system and of the London exchange, the rupee was practically controlled by the price of silver.

Until England placed a restriction on the sale of Indian Council Bills in December, 1916[1] and, subsequently, in August, November and December, 1917,[2] trade with India was financed through the purchase of these Council Bills at London.[3] Japan alone needed to buy 150 to 170 million rupees worth of Council Bills per year, for her net excess of imports from India was over 100 million yen per year against which very little of non-visible receipts was expected in favor of Japan.

JAPAN'S TRADE WITH INDIA DURING THE WAR[4]

(million yen)

	Exports	*Imports*	*Excess of imports*	*Total*
1914	26	160	−134	
1915	42	147	−105	
1916	71	179	−107	−533
1917	101	223	−122	
1918	202	268	−65	

[1] The sale was limited to 8 million rupees per week.

[2] Between December 1916 and August 1917, the issue was increased. But in August 1917, again, it was limited to 9 million rupees, and so in November 1917 to 6 million rupees, and in December to 4 million rupees per week. Chief reasons for these restrictions were (1) silver reserve of India treasury as well as gold standard reserve went very low and on the other hand the currency was greatly increased in India. (2) Flotation of domestic bonds in India was not successful because Indians hoarded much silver. (3) Silver became scarce and high in price.

[3] In order to pay rupees to Indian exporters of cotton, the Japanese importer's banker had to buy, through London, Council bills which were offered weekly for bid and which when sent to Calcutta, Bombay, or Madras, were payable in Indian Currency or silver.

[4] Department of Finance, *Kinyu Jikō*, 1925, p. 222.

Japan needed Indian cotton and imported such an amount [1] that she had to effect the payment of many hundreds of million yen to India every year. Up to and through 1916, Japan could manage (1) to buy Council Bills at London, (2) to buy up export bills on India in China and the South Seas, (3) to purchase Indian securities, (4) and to ship gold and silver to India,[2] thus directly building up funds in India to finance the trade. But after September, 1917 when America put an embargo on gold and silver and the India office put a most severe restriction on Council Bills in December of that same year, there were almost no means left for the Japanese with which to buy cotton from India. Japan had money in New York, so she was able up to September, 1917 to import gold from the United States and to re-ship it to India. In

[1] Japan's imports of Indian raw cotton as recorded by the British India Government were as follows. Notice that more than 75 per. cent of India's cotton went to Japan. *Statistical Abstract for British India from 1915-16 to 1924-25*, London, 1926, pp. 490-491.

JAPAN'S IMPORTS OF INDIAN RAW COTTON
(in million Rs.)

	1915	*1916*	*1917*	*1918*	*1919*	*1920*	*1921*	*1922*	*1923*	*1924*
To Japan	170	259	307	233	412	205	325	344	426	458
India's total exports	249	361	426	309	586	416	539	709	984	912

[2] The specie movement with India was as follows (Department of Finance, *Kinyu Jikō Sankosho*, Tokio, 1924, pp. 234-240).

SPECIE MOVEMENT WITH INDIA
(million yen)

	Exports to India		*Imports from India*		*Total excess of exports or imports (–)*
	gold	*silver*	*gold*	*silver*	
1914	–	–	–	–	–
1915	–	–	14	–	–14
1916	2	2	6	–	–2
1917	100	2	–	–	102
1918	–	–	–	–	–

1917 alone more than 100 million yen worth of gold was re-shipped to India. But after September, when Japan put an embargo on gold and silver after the American fashion, the problem of financing the Japanese-Indian trade became intensified, and especially after the Seiyukai, the opposition party, seized this economic problem as a political issue against the existing government.

The Seiyukai's stand was that out of Japan's total import of 670 million pounds of cotton, one-half should be imported from America, so that the net payment to India would be lessened to 20 million yen per year, which should be sent in gold specie out of the 460 million yen stock of gold which then Japan held at home, and that for this amount the government should grant a special permit. But the government's position was different. In the eyes of the government 460 million yen gold was absolutely necessary at home in order to safeguard the increasing note issue, as the Japanese had no means to replenish the gold reserve after the American gold embargo. As to the means for financing cotton, the government favored (1) to offer ships to be chartered in India and to send more freighters to India and the South Seas for their service, thus aiming at more invisible receipts. (2) The government also favored handling more Java sugar and transporting it to India, as that country was greatly short of sugar. Both means were tried. Fortunately, both came out successfully. Free chartering was permitted by the government, and many ships were chartered. Thus, Japanese steamers plying the South Seas and Indian Ocean became numerous. Java sugar was also soon manipulated by the Japanese. It is estimated that in 1918 Mitsui & Co., Furukawa & Co., and Suzuki & Co. alone shipped more than 55 million yen worth of sugar to India.[1] Now the government could expect more than 80 million yen from these

[1] K. Maeda, *ibid.*, p. 173.

sources, and the rest was easily to be relied on in Council Bills. Such was the brief history of Japanese-Indian finance. The ease or difficulty of such financing together with prices of silver were well reflcted in the Japanese-Indian exchange. During 1914, 1915 and 1916 financial difficulties were less; and although exchanges on Bombay and Calcutta fluctuated as widely as 6 rupees at one time, in the main the exchange remained normal. In 1917 payments were effected by gold shipments. But in 1918 when the financial and silver situations became most gloomy, the exchange dropped an average of 12 rupees from that of 1917, or the value of yen rapidly decreased. As an example, the course of Bombay exchange may be here cited together with the prices of silver and the trade.

RATES OF EXCHANGE ON BOMBAY DURING THE WAR

(Rupees per Y 100.00)

	high	*low*	*average*	*trade* [1]	*Silver* [2]
1914	153.250	151.500	152.140	−134	54
1915	158.500	151.500	154.646	−105	49
1916	159.250	156.500	147.521	−107	65
1917	157.750	144.500	150.787	−122	81
1918	154.500	107.500	138.221	—65	96

Thus it shows that, in general, pegging the Indian exchange in Japan was successful until 1918 by utilizing New York exchange facilities, and after the American gold and silver embargo, by dealing through direct barter. But the rise of silver beginning with 1917 [3] and in 1918 was effective in

[1] Excess of imports by Japan from India in millions of yen; *vide supra*, p. 86.

[2] Average price of silver in cents per fine ounce in New York; *vide supra*, p. 83.

[3] At the time of the Pitman Act of April 1918, the price of silver seemed to have reached the top, but in reality and in result the act aided the rising movement of silver, and in December 1919, it reached its maximum.

raising the Indian exchange in spite of the fact that the trade in 1918 was better balanced than in former years, showing conclusively that the price of silver was the dominant factor in determining the Japanese-Indian exchange just as in the case of Chinese-Japanese exchange.

10. PROBLEMS OF FINANCING FOREIGN TRADE

As the War went on, the growth of Japan's trade was simply marvelous. Both her exports and her invisible receipts were multiplying by leaps and bounds. The total net credits for each of these years were as follows:

	1914	*1915*	*1916*	*1917*	*1918*	*Total*
Visible trade	2	191	417	618	338	1,566
Invisible trade ...	-6	69	277	415	578	1,333
Total credit ...	-4	260	694	1,033	916	2,899

With this enormous accumulation of credit, Japan had to meet two great financial problems. One was how to finance foreign trade at home; the other was how to use the funds accumulated abroad.

Taking up the first problem: how to finance foreign trade at home. The situation created by the War was this: because export bills far outbalanced import bills by hundreds of millions of yen and because exchange rates were pegged, exchange bankers could no longer finance foreign trade either by balancing import and export bills, nor by the use of their own capitals and reserves as in ordinary times. Then, consider that there was no discount market, no great use of bank acceptances, and no coordination between domestic and foreign trade financing. For small amounts, exchange bankers might have been able to borrow on long-term contract; but for tens and hundreds of millions of yen, they had to resort to the call-loan market. But to borrow money from a call-loan market and invest it in two months' or four months' export bills was, of course, not always profitable, especially when demand for short money was persistent and interest was high.[1] Yet the banks, like the Yokohama Specie Bank, had to resort to this practice when no other means were available.

The next source to which exchange bankers turned was the Bank of Japan. Now the Bank of Japan was willing to loan exchange funds at low rates of interest, but was required by the Bank Regulation to have securities for such loans; and before 1919 there was no method whereby exchange bankers could discount their export bills without presenting such securities or collaterals. Even so, the loans made for exchange bills were enormous as the war went on and the exchange funds at home became exceedingly tight. This was especially the case after the American embargo, for Japanese bankers could no longer import gold. Indeed, in those last two years it seemed as if the chief business of the Bank of Japan was to finance trade by loaning on foreign exchange bills; for over 70 per cent of the total loans were made for such purposes, as the following statistics show.

Still another method by which bankers could finance trade was to import gold and silver. In 1916 net specie imports were 72 million yen, and in 1917, 238 million yen, and in 1918 only 4 million yen, showing that after September, 1917 financing by gold mports became impossible. Exchange banks were also financing export trade by selling Japanese foreign bonds as well as foreign bonds which they obtained abroad. But in Japan when industries were prosperous people did not like to invest in bonds. So this had also a set

[1] The interest rates in New York were around 4 to 5 per cent while in Japan the rates were more than 7 to 8 per cent. Naturally exchange bankers hated to borrow dear money in Japan and to invest in the cheap New York market.

LOANS OF THE BANK OF JAPAN DURING THE WAR[1]

(in millions of yen)

Year	Month	Loans on Foreign Exchange Bills	All other loans	Total	Percentage of loans on Foreign Exchange Bills to total loans
1914	6	33	45	78	42%
	12	46	41	87	52
1915	6	6	13	19	31
	12	20	38	58	34
1916	6	24	17	41	58
	12	120	68	188	63
1917	6	120	57	177	67
	12	199	73	272	73
1918	6	232	77	309	75
	12	444	132	576	78

limit. It was done only approximately to the extent of 300 million yen. Meanwhile, exchange bankers were eagerly asking the government for help, for it was a risky business to carry such a large fund abroad at a time when exchange was not stabilized. Thereupon the Okuma Cabinet after 1915 issued domestic bonds several times, the proceeds of which were used to buy the bankers' foreign exchange funds and ultimately to meet the redemption of government's foreign bonds. These approximately amounted to 260 million yen during the War. The government was also successful in inducing a group of bankers to form a syndicate to subscribe to foreign loans amounting for the last four years to 650 million yen. These were all to reduce the amount of trade credits created abroad. Yet funds were accumulating in the hands of exchange bankers. So the government used most of the Deposit Section's money,[2] and surpluses of General

[1] Based on Department of Finance, *Kinyu Jikō Sankosho*, 1925, pp. 87-88.

[2] The Deposit Section is a bureau in the Department of Finance to take

Account [1] to buy up these funds in London and New York. Not only that, but the government, when the Teauchi cabinet came into existence in October, 1916, stopped the policy of domestic loans for fear of high prices, and instead began to issue treasury bills,[2] the proceeds of which were used partly to finance the munition export bills for the Allies and partly to buy the exchange funds. It is generally estimated that over 150 million yen were used for such exchange purposes.[3] Thus, the bankers were able to get funds at home and reduce the funds abroad. The Bank of Japan, too, besides loaning on foreign exchange bills, helped the exchange bankers by buying up exchange funds abroad, amounting to 130 million yen, which was turned in to the Bank's agents abroad, and advanced an equal sum of notes to them at home.[4] This was considered as an unusual, unprecedented case

These various methods of financing have relieved the exchange bankers a great deal. But in view of the enormous increase of exports and freight, these means were not alto-

care of deposits of Post Office and of deposits transferred from Special Account. Deposits of Post Office were: (million yen)

1914	*1915*	*1916*	*1917*	*1918*
206	235	314	438	589

[1] Japan's budget is composed of two parts: General Account and Special Account. Special Account is for government's industrial undertakings and for colonial finances. Surpluses of General Account were as follows: (*The 25th Financial and Economic Annual of Japan*, Government Printing Office, 1925, p. 17) (in millions of yen)

	1914	*1915*	*1916*	*1917*	*1918*
Surplus of General Account	86	125	222	349	462

[2] Issued according to the Regulation of Temporary Treasury Bills of July, 1917.

[3] K. Maeda, *A Study of Yen Exchange*, 1925, p. 186.

[4] J. Inoue, *Japan's International Finance*, Tokio, 1926, p. 40.

gether satisfactory. So the government, impressed by the seriousness of the situation, formed the War Exchange Adjustment Committee to which representatives of business men, bankers and government officials were appointed. They met in the latter part of September, 1918 and recommended the following policy: [1]

1. To issue more Temporary Treasury Bills; but the method of such issue should be improved.
2. To favor foreign investments and to investigate such opportunities.
3. To buy exporters' export bills with Temporary Treasury Bills.
4. To lower the rate of interest.
5. To try to balance exports and imports as much as possible.
6. Government control of foreign exchange.
7. To mobilize all the Japanese bonds in America.
8. To have better financial connection between Bank of Japan and Federal Reserve Bank of New York.
9. To induce America to export more gold and silver.
10. To favor permanent organization of the Exchange Adjustment Committee.
11. To sponsor the Conference of Japanese and American Bankers.

But these measures had been already tried, and there was nothing new about these proposals. As a matter of fact, there was a fundamental dilemma. On the one hand, the government wanted to keep down the dollar exchange in order to encourage exports; on the other hand, the government wanted to protect exchange bankers by checking any further increase of funds abroad, as such accumulation was

[1] J. Inoue, *ibid.*, pp. 47-50.

risky [1] to the bankers in view of the tendency that the dollar exchange might be raised more. It was really the duty of the government either to let exchange rates rise freely so that further exports would be curtailed and imports encouraged, or to try to safeguard the exchange funds by pegging the dollar exchange down.

Both the Okuma and Terauchi cabinets were unable to solve his important problem, and in September, 1918 the Hara cabinet came into existence. Now the government abandoned the whole traditional policy of encouraging exports and of repressing imports. It abolished the artificial means of pegging exchanges. But instead, the government installed the so-called free policy of exchange; that is, to let exports pay imports or vice versa, and to let exchanges act or be acted on accordingly.

In changing the policy of the government, the Department of Finance issued in essence the following statement on October 16, 1918:

Whereas Japan's financial balance to the world is not only based on the excess of exports but also freight, insurance premium, etc., and whereas this balance is increasing year after year, to stick to the old policy of encouraging exports and to let the Yokohama Specie Bank and other exchange banks maintain such rates which would be favorable to exporters and which are below those of foreign branch banks, would naturally put all import bills in the hands of foreign bankers and would thereby put our exchange bankers in a one-sided transaction and soon put them out of their own funds. To continue such practice has not only induced inflation but has also caused a great loss, for as there was at one time as big a spread as $2.00 between

[1] For instance, even a rise of 2 points in the exchange on the fund of 300 million yen would be a loss of approximately $375,000. The exchange funds held by bankers alone were more than 500 million yen in New York. J. Inoue, *ibid.*, p. 46.

our bankers' rates and those of foreign bankers, even the exporters of Shanghai and Dairen drew their export bills to New York through Japan. Therefore, in order to adjust the situation, the government is now favoring a raise of the exchange rates to a more natural state, but not so much as to impair our exports to any appreciable amount.

But again, this policy was not adequate to meet the given situation, for such a policy of raising rates may be applicable when exchange funds were small in amount, but at this time when exchange bankers had over 500 million yen abroad[1] any more rise of exchange was a threat to them; besides the handling of important bills—even if exchange bankers could handle all such import bills—would not have amounted to much, for supposing the government by the enforcement of the new policy should have 20 per cent more imports and 20 per cent less exports, the debit balance would then be only 67 million yen in three months, or it would take 25 months more to offset above 500 million yen. The account may be illustrated as follows:

MONTHLY TRADE OF 1918
(million yen)

	Exports		Imports		Excess (— = excess of imports)	
	Actual	20% less	Actual	20% more	Actual	20% calculation
October...	186	149	126	151	60	—2
November.	182	146	152	182	30	—36
December.	207	166	163	195	46	—29
						—67

[1] J. Inoue, *ibid.*, p. 46; K. Maeda, *ibid.*, p. 202.

Therefore, it was natural that the government's exchange policy, being inapplicable, came to a deadlock. Meanwhile, unexpectedly on November 11, 1918 came the Armistice. As the War in July, 1914 rescued Japan from the financial deadlock caused by many years' successive over-imports, so the Armistice again saved Japan from the financial deadlock caused by the successive over-exports, for with the Armistice came the general change of level of prices followed by the monthly excesses of imports, and the lifting of the embargo on silver in April and on gold in June, 1919 by America, relieved the situation, the details of which will be discussed in the next chapter.

II. SUMMARY

Before we come to the next period, however, a brief summary at this point may help to make clear to the mind of the reader what was the exchange situation in Japan before 1919.

In the first place, prices were moving relatively less fast in Japan than abroad. Higher prices abroad were, of course, due to the War. The war caused, on the commodity side, relatively less production and relatively greater demand, and, on the money side, a greater inflation. Japan contributed a part by supplying needs not only in the European and American continents but also in the Orient where European goods were practically cut off. The result was a great excess of exports together with an enormous amount of invisible trade receipts. In five years the trade increased three times and invisible receipts almost five times. The country was very prosperous. The industrial expansion was two and one-half times more than the pre-war condition. The Japanese exchange, however, was pegged to remain at a little below par by means of the exchange fund system until September, 1915, when a further increase in the excess of exports made exchanges rise above par. Of course, up to this time the exchange on London was the standard exchange in Japan.. So the abnormal fall of exchange on New York in Japan at that time, it was thought, was due to the fall of sterling exchange in New York. But with the beginning of 1916, the New York exchange replaced the London exchange and virtually became the standard of all foreign exchanges. And the rising tendency of Japanese yen exchange on New York was due to Japan's piling up of balances at New York. This tendency is fully shown by the accompanying Chart III. First, we see the upward movement of American prices followed by Japanese prices. This fact is illustrated by the high purchasing power parity of the yen against the dollar. This gave a favorable balance of payments which is exemplified and shown by a trend of favorable balance of commodity trade. And finally, the trend of exchange went up. But toward the latter half of 1917 and throughout 1918, when the trend of Japanese prices went up steeply, the trend of the purchasing power parity went down, causing thereafter less exports. But contrary to the expectation of the result of these movements, the yen exchange on New York went up still higher due to the abnormal accumulation of exchange funds in New York. All these movements may be seen in Chart III.[1]

In the second place, the rise in the price of silver was the controlling factor in the fall of Japanese exchange on China and later in the Japanese exchange on India, showing that in those trades the exchange was an influencing factor and not the balance of payments. That is to say that 100 yen which were worth 88 taels in the beginning of the War were now worth only 42 taels at the end of the War when the price of silver rose from *d*23 to *d*48 in the corresponding period,

[1] The sources of this chart are found from those tables already given.

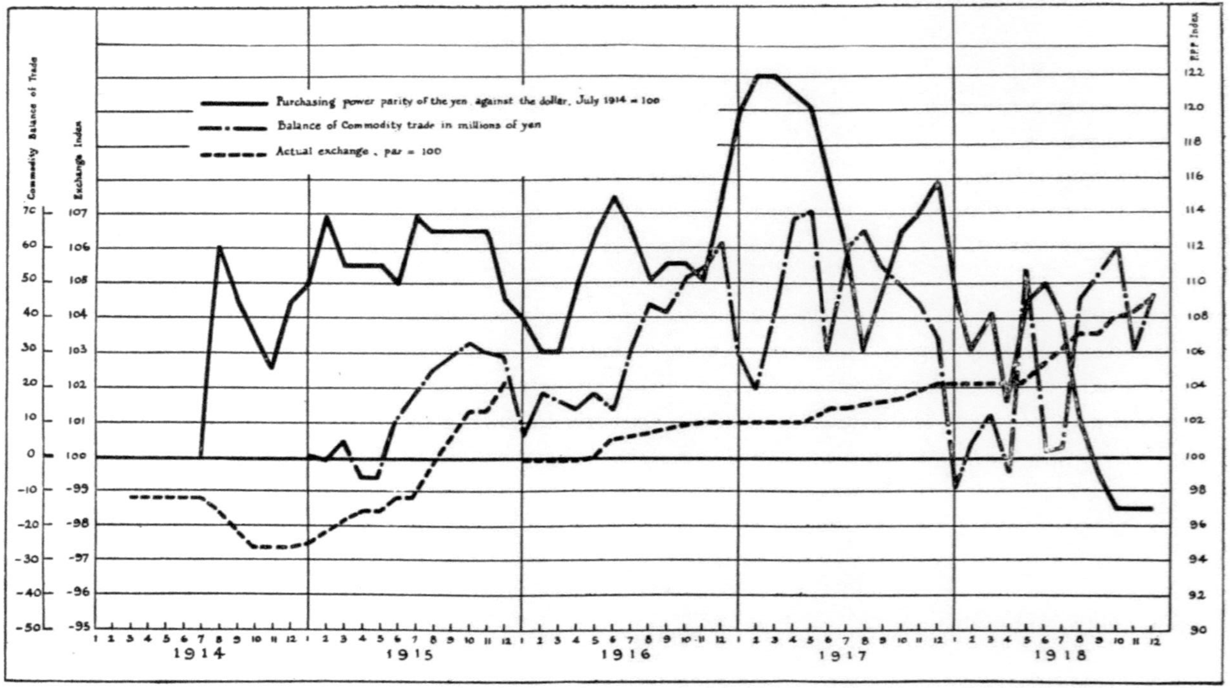

CHART III. PURCHASING POWER PARITY, BALANCE OF TRADE AND EXCHANGES DURING THE WAR
(During 1914-15 London exchanges, after 1916 New York exchanges are used)

while the balance of payments between China and Japan was always in favor of Japan, commodity trade alone being Japan's excess of exports from 50 to 200 million yen every year. This, however, does not mean to deny that the altered moving pars were eventually effected through the current balance of payments. But the point is that if it were not due to high rates of the tael, Japanese imports from China would have been much larger in quantity and less in value, especially in 1918.[1]

In the third place, the degree of Japan's dependence on the London discount market and later on the New York discount and free gold markets was well evidenced by such events as the restriction of Council Bills, of gold movements, the shifting of exchange funds from London to New York, the American gold embargo, etc. On the other hand, Japan's lack of adequate means of financing trade and adjusting exchanges was also clearly shown at this time when things were already in Japan's favor.

[1] *Vide supra*, pp. 82-83 for the Chino-Japanese trade.

CHAPTER IV

Yen Exchange and the Balance of Payments After the War, 1919-1923

1. GENERAL OUTLOOK AFTER THE WAR

THE general economic situation in Japan immediately after the War, 1919-1923, was characterized by three movements. The first was the price movement. After 1919 prices in Japan were moving relatively higher than those of Great Britain and America, reaching a peak in March, 1920, followed by a panic which caused various war-nursed industries to close their doors one after another during the remainder of the period. The second was the trade movement. After 1919 Japan's trade was completely reversed and each year saw an excess of imports. During the War Japan earned in trade 1,292 million yen; but after the War, 1919-1923, she lost 2,486 million yen. The third was the exhaustion of Japan's gold funds held abroad. On January 1, 1919 she held 1,135 million yen abroad; but this amount decreased in December 31, 1923 to 444 million yen. Results were persistently unfavorable to the Japanese exchanges. And the government's pegging policy proved to be a complete failure, while at home credit control was totally lacking. The true sequence of these movements in the long-run analysis seems to have been, first, the expansion of credit, then, the movement of rising prices following by great excess of imports, and lastly, the fall of exchanges.

In order to understand the working of this reversal in economic conditions, let me elucidate a little more, step by step.

2. RISE IN PRICES

In the first place, there were several ways by which the volume of bank notes was increased in Japan after 1919. The first was by the increase in the amount of gold reserve through specie importation. We have already seen that Japan was worrying much about her accumulation of gold and exchange funds in New York, because the Japanese were fearing the decline of New York exchange rates and the loss of interest. But when America lifted her gold embargo in June, 1919, Japan soon began to import gold heavily.[1] And this naturally reenforced the gold reserve of the Bank of Japan. It had been the opinion of government officials that no inflation could take place so long as the percentage of gold cover had not been lowered. Certainly the percentage was not lowered but greatly raised,[2] especially during 1920 and 1921 when gold imports were heavy. But this was by no means a guaranty against inflation. Another practice which helped to increase this percentage of gold reserve was through the inclusion among the Bank's reserves of gold funds held abroad by the Bank of Japan, a practice which continued for a long time, in fact until September 30, 1922. On the whole, no country had increased its gold-reserve relatively more than Japan did after the War. The Federal Reserve Bulletin in America reports as follows:

[1] Japan's gold imports after the War may be seen here (Department of Finance, *The 25th Financial and Economic Annual of Japan*, Tokio, 1926, pp. 146-7).

JAPAN'S GOLD IMPORTS AFTER THE WAR
(million yen)

	Exports	Imports	Excess of imports	Total net imports
1919	5	327	322	
1920	3	404	400	
1921	—	138	138	860

[2] *Vide supra*, p. 28.

GOLD RESERVES OF THE PRINCIPAL COUNTRIES AFTER THE WAR[1]
(million dollars)

	Gold holdings			Per cent of world supply		
	1913	1918	1921	1913	1918	1921
U. S. A.	491	2,245	2,529	21.7	37.7	37.0
U. K.	170	523	763	5.3	8.8	11.1
France	678	664	688	21.3	11.1	10.0
Germany	278	538	260	8.7	9.0	3.8
Japan	64	225	558	2.0	3.7	8.1

The second way by which notes were unduly increased was by the issuance of government railroad bonds and treasury bills and the fact that these were soon discounted at the central bank.[2]

The third channel was the issuance of fractional currency of 10, 20, 50 *sen* notes directly by the government. This was started during the War in November, 1917 when such small denominations of money were needed. And the government kept issuing them until the outstanding volume became finally enormous.[3]

[1] Federal Reserve *Bulletin*, June 1921, p. 676.

[2] *Vide supra*, p. 28. The government and other bonds have always exceeded the amount of commercial paper.

[3] The increase of government's fractional paper was as follows: (Department of Finance, *Kinyu Jikō*, pp. 2-4.

INCREASE OF GOVERNMENT'S FRACTIONAL PAPER
(million yen)

At the end of		Outstanding
I	1917	19
	1918	91
II	1919	145
	1920	200
	1921	216
	1922	158
	1923	68

While central authorities believed faithfully in the old superstition that gold cover was the true basis of the value of a currency and did not question seriously the *relative amount of means of payment,* but kept on issuing notes on gold, the local bankers, much impressed and intoxicated by the war-boom, instead of contracting their credits, expanded their loans without taking any heed to the price movement, the form, relative amount, or objects for which such loans were made. For credits advanced by the Special Banks, by the Ordinary Banks and Savings Banks after the war as compared with the pre-war period (taking 1912-1913 as 100) increased to 344, 422, 634 respectively, or an average increase of 466, the figures of which may be seen below.

EXPANSION OF BANK CREDIT IN JAPAN[1]

(in million yen)

At the end of	Special Banks		Ordinary Banks		Savings Banks	
	Amount	Average and (Index)	Amount	Average and (Index)	Amount	Average and (Index)
I { 1912	769		1,522		232	
1913	816	782 (100)	1,670	1,586 (100)	261	246 (100)
II { 1914	806		1,726		293	
1915	830		1,728		437	
1916	1,093		2,232		514	
1917	1,484		2,987		669	
1918	2,334	1,309 (167)	4,146	2,562 (161)	952	571 (232)
III { 1919	2,748		5,666		1,466	
1920	2,239		5,902		1,597	
1921	2,686		6,241		1,618	1,560
1922	2,948		7,779		*186	(634)
1923	2,752	2,694 (344)	7,956	6,708 (422)	*202	

[1] Calculated from Department of Finance, *Kinyu Jikō*, 1925, pp. 80-84 and *The 25th Financial and Economic Annual of Japan*, 1925, pp. 128-133. These figures include total outstanding balances made for loans and bills discounted. Notice the rapid increase after 1918.

* The decrease here is due to the enactment of Savings Banks law.

But trade did not increase with such a rapidity. For instance, the foreign trade only increased from the pre-war period from 100 to 262, as seen below. And in domestic

RELATIVE INCREASE OF VOLUME OF TRADE

	Foreign Trade		Domestic Trade		
	Amount	Average and Index	Rice Average value and Index	Raw Silk[1] Actual value and Index	Cotton yarn[2] Actual value and Index
I {1912–1913.}	......	1,320	1,050	206	191
		(100)	(100)	(100)	(100)
II {1914–1918.}	......	2,501	1,008	546	598
		(189)	(96)	(265)	(313)
III {1919–1923.}	......	3,467	2,183	813	628
		(262)	(208)	(399)	(328)

COTTON YARN PRODUCTION AFTER THE WAR

	Production	Prices	Total Amount
	million bales	Y per bale	million yen
1913	1.3	147	191
1918	1.7	352	598
1919	1.9	428	813
1920	1.8	449	808
1921	1.8	262	471
1922	2.2	239	528
1923	2.1	248	520

trade, in rice production, the increase was only 208, in raw silk 399, and in cotton yarn 328, each of which is far below

[1] These are five years averages based on Reports of the Department of Agriculture and Forestry, pp. 179, 189.

[2] The production of cotton yarn in millions of bales and their yearly average prices were as follows (*The Japan Year Book for 1926*, Tokio, 1926, p. 295 and Department of Finance, *Kinyu Jikō*, 1924, p. 312).

the credit expansion of 466. Thus our statistical analysis clearly shows that much credit was used merely for speculative purposes.

Aside from these notes and credit expansions which caused high prices, there were also extravagant government expenditures and nursed speculation, all of which helped to enhance prices. In government expenditures Japan spent after the War nearly twice as many yen as she spent during the War; that is, 197 per cent more than the war period, or an increase of 22 per cent on the basis of the purchasing power of money.[1] The object here is to show that the yearly in-

[1] Following is the settled accounts of the State Revenue and Expenditure of General Account (excluding Special Account).

JAPAN'S ANNUAL REVENUE AND EXPENDITURE *
(million yen)

Fiscal Year		Revenue			Expenditure			Expenditure of 5 years average and Index number	Surplus
		Ordinary	Extra-ordinary	Total	Ordinary	Extra-ordinary	Total		
I	1909	483	194	667	394	138	532		144
	1910	491	181	672	421	157	569		103
	1911	508	148	657	409	175	585		71
	1912	552	135	687	416	176	593		93
	1913	575	146	721	415	157	573	570 (100)	148
II	1914	536	198	734	399	249	648		86
	1915	638	169	708	386	196	583		125
	1916	622	191	813	386	204	590		222
	1917	763	321	1,084	427	297	735		349
	1918	911	567	1,379	490	526	1,017	712 (124)	462
III	1919	1,063	745	1,808	502	669	1,172		636
	1920	1,174	825	2,000	709	650	1,359		640
	1921	1,283	781	2,065	841	648	1,489		575
	1922	1,428	559	2,087	891	438	1,429		657
	1923	1,303	741	2,045	960	560	1,521	1,394 (244)	524

* *Department of Financial and Economic Annual of Japan*, 1925, p. 17.

crease in the state expenditure was faster than the movement of prices, and was a cause which had contributed to enhance the general level of prices. High prices, then, assisted in the swelling of the state expenditure.

Extravagance was seen in the expenditures of not only central government but also of local governments, such as prefectural, municipal and village governments. These expenditures trebled during the post-war period when compared with those of the war period. Even on the basis of the purchasing power of money, the increase was more than 61 per cent.[1] And although the population was increasing dur-

The average price index for the periods of I, II and III, were 100, 129 and 218 respectively. The Revenue and Expenditure of Special Account (where Government keeps industrial, certain military, colonial, certain educational, social, and other special accounts) have been as follows:

JAPAN'S SPECIAL ACCOUNT AFTER THE WAR †

	1919	1920	1921	1922	1923
Revenue	2.688	3,043	3,208	3,407	3,322
Expenditure	1,908	2,265	2,391	3,135	3,011
Surplus	780	778	807	272	311

† Figures for 1922 and 1923 are budget figures and not settled accounts. Department of Finance, *Kinyu Jikō*, 1924, p. 133.

[1] Following are calculated from *Interior Department's Statistics*, pp. 160-61. (See table on opposite page, "Local Government Revenue.")

ing the period, the real increase of tax burden per head since 1912-13 was over 12 per cent, as the following figures show.

INCREASE OF TAX BURDEN AFTER THE WAR[1]

		Tax per head	Average	Index number of Prices	Real increase of tax burden
I	1912	Y 9.1	Y 9. (100)	100	0%
	1913	8.9			
II	1914	8.8	10.1 (112)	129	—4%
	1915	8.3			
	1916	8.9			
	1917	10.6			
	1918	14.2			
III	1919	20.1	22. (244)	218	12%
	1920	20.8			
	1921	22.5			
	1922	24.6			
	1923	..			

LOCAL GOVERNMENT REVENUE AND EXPENDITURE
(million yen)

		Revenue	Expenditure	Average	Surplus	Index number of prices: Average for each period	Real Expenditure
I	1912	375	320	315 (100)	55	100	100
	1913	356	310		46		
II	1914	354	310	354 (112)	44	129	86 (100)
	1915	347	300		47		
	1916	367	317		50		
	1917	459	366		93		
	1918	571	480		91		
III	1919	785	631	961 (305)	154	218	139 (161)
	1920	1,114	915		199		
	1921	1,286	1,034		252		
	1922	1,121	1,100		21		
	1923	1,141	1,128		13		

[1] Department of Finance, *Kinyu Jikō Sankosho*, 1925, p. 143.

These expenditures of central and local governments, therefore, not only increased taxes and thereby enhanced prices, but more effectually did so by increasing bonds; and the bonds were soon discounted at banks. The increase of these government bonds was as follows:

INCREASE OF CENTRAL GOVERNMENTS'S DOMESTIC BONDS [1]
(in millions of yen)

I	1914....	1,036	II 1919....	1,483
	1915....	1,021	1920....	1,686
	1916....	1,097	1921....	2,149
	1917....	1,156	1922....	2,363
	1918....	1,211	1923....	2,555

INCREASE OF LOCAL GOVERNMENTS' BONDS [2]
(in millions of yen)

	At the end of	Amount		At the end of	Amount	Per head obligation (Y)
I	1914....	327	II	1919....	342	5.98
	1915....	337		1920....	379	6.55
	1916....	334		1921....	467	7.97
	1917....	336		1922....	557	9.38
	1918....	337		1923....	676	11.56

On the other hand, the great war-prosperity seemed to have given an idea to the people that whoever engaged in export trade or manufacturing enterprises was sure to make profits. And this idea pushed to other industries, even to real-estate dealings in a remote countryside. While the main productive forces of the country were largely directed to export industries, speculation was so widespread that when the war stopped there was not much left in the way of commodities for home consumption, and this condition of

[1] Bank of Japan, *Economic Statistics of Japan*, Tokio, 1925, pp. 46-48.

[2] Compiled by Nippon Kogyo Ginko, *cf. ibid.*, p. 51.

scarcity pushed prices still higher. However, after April 1920, these war-fed industries and business enterprises began to liquidate one after another and this finally caused the panic of 1920.[1] This can well be illustrated by the high percentage of dishonored bills due to industrial failures during the year and the rest of the period.[2]

When prices were rising, and orders were coming in, money and credits were in turn recklessly extended during the war and up to March, 1920. Profits and dividends were so enormous that the rate of interest soon rose; and the Bank of Japan was obliged to raise its own discount rates twice in the latter part of 1918 and twice again in the latter part of 1919[3] as the average market discount rate in Japan

[1] J. Inoue, *Japan's Economic and Financial Situation after the War*, Tokio, 1925, pp. 29-45.

[2] The source of following figures: Department of Finance, *Kinyu Jikō*, 1924, pp. 115-116.

DISHONORED BILLS AFTER THE WAR
(million yen)

		Amount	Amount cleared	Percentage to the total clearance
I	1912	.7	9,712	.077
	1913	.7	10,401	.073
II	1914	.7	10,269	.071
	1915	.4	11,625	.038
	1016	.3	20,234	.018
	1917	.8	31,789	.027
	1918	1.3	53,414	.025
III	1919	2.3	77,109	.030
	1920	6.2	74,068	.084
	1921	4.4	68,232	.065
	1922	5.2	71,813	.073
	1923	4.2	68,185	.063

[3] On September 15, 1918, the Bank raised its discount rate for com-

was over 8.4 per cent, the maximum rate being over 10 per cent. All corporations both old and new increased their capital for extension and promotion, reaching the peak in 1920. However, when a sharp depression of prices came in March, 1920, these swollen industries began to be squeezed down miserably, resulting in more frequent business and bank failures. This reversed condition may be well seen by the following figures. Notice the rapid growth up to 1920 and the sudden decline after 1921.

CAPITAL FOR PROMOTION AND EXTENSION OF ALL CORPORATIONS [1]
(million yen)

Industries	1914	1915	1916	1917	1918	1919	1920	1921	1922	1923
Manufacturing	40	107	310	586	878	1029	1758	473	249	384
Shipping	51	77	84	223	311	453	534	349	244	238
Agricultural	3	1	3	25	35	178	184	117	16	5
Commercial	35	27	43	192	621	611	1172	444	329	252
Electric	30	41	75	92	155	460	196	372	293	330
Others	....	....	....	....	....	....	....	....	....	....
Total	250	292	658	1562	2676	4068	5113	2236	1491	1482

In Japan the price movement was really a predominating force in controlling the fate of all industries, trade and banking. Our price chart, Chart IV, shows that the period was marked by a sharp rise of prices during 1919, reaching the highest peak in March, 1920, followed by an even sharper depression; and then, prices remained for the rest of the

mercial papers from 5.11% to 5.84%; and on November 25, it again raised to 6.57%; and on October 6, 1919, it raised to 7.3% and again on November 19 up to 8.03%. (Bank of Japan, *Economic Statistics of Japan*, Tokio, 1925, p. 35.)

[1] These figures represent capitals of new corporations and the increased capitals of old corporations. They are not total capitals of all corporations in Japan. Source, Bank of Japan, *Economic Statistics of Japan*, Tokio, 1925, p. 46.

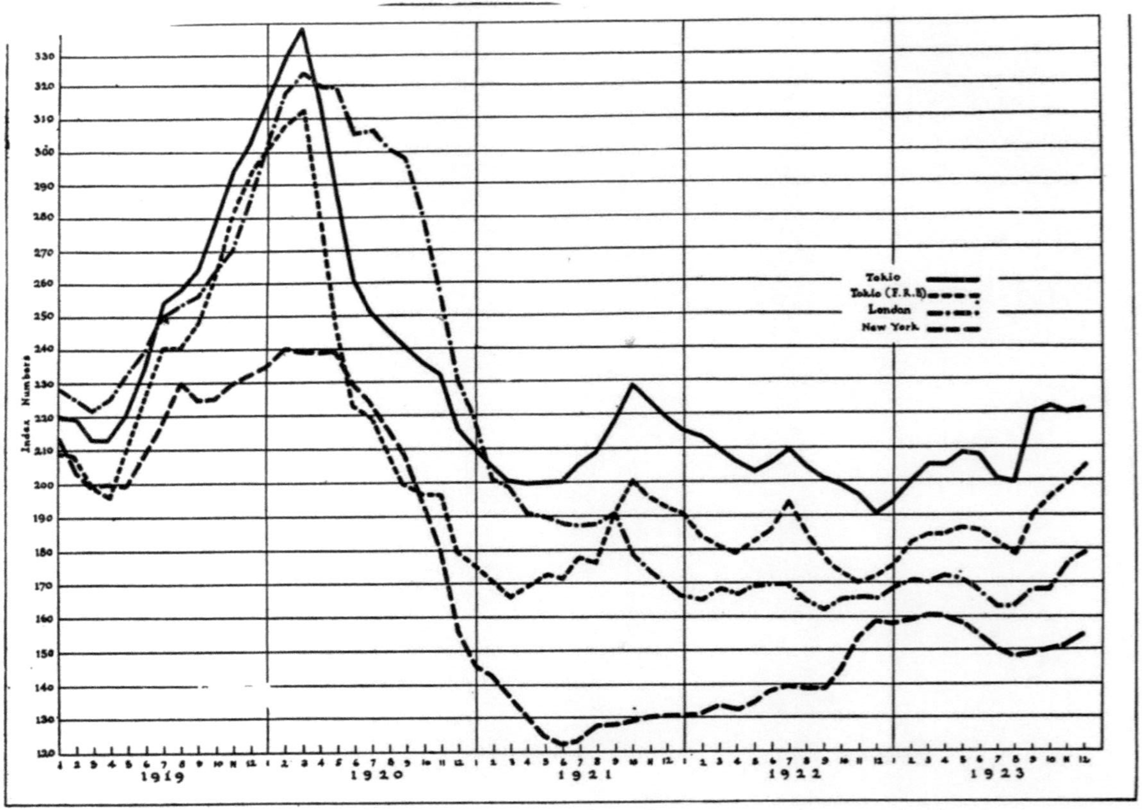

CHART IV. TOKIO, LONDON AND NEW YORK WHOLESALE PRICES AFTER THE WAR
(July 1914 = 10

period at a relatively higher level than those of Great Britain or America.[1] On the gold basis, too, Japanese prices were much higher than those of the British Isles or America.

WHOLESALE PRICE INDEX ON GOLD BASIS [2]

	U. S. A.	England	Japan
1913	100	100	100
1919	211	219	241
1920	239	233	242
1921	149	156	175
1922	158	150	175
1923	164	159	183

In the depression of March, 1920, one thing cannot escape notice. That is that, while the same kind of depression took place all over the world, the Japanese depression came somewhat earlier and was sharper than those in other important countries.[3] This earlier and sharper depression, as far as Japanese markets were concerned, was first led by the depression of the raw silk market which came in January of that year. To illustrate, a year ago, in January, 1919 the highest quotation for raw silk (shinshu No. 1) in Yokohama was Y. 1,520 per bale. This steadily increased during the year, and in December it was Y. 3,280. A year later, in January, 1920 it reached the highest peak with Y. 4,350. Then, the New York market first went down, followed by

[1] *See* accompanying Chart IV. There are certain technical objections to the Bank of Japan's index number. So I have also plotted in this chart a dotted line for Japanese prices based on the Federal Reserve Board's Annual Report, 1924, pp. 163-165. For similar chart, *see* Federal Reserve Board, *Prices in the United States and Abroad, 1919-1923*, Washington, 1924, p. 3. Other sources, same as Chart I.

[2] Federal Reserve *Bulletin*, September, 1922, pp. 1054-1055.

[3] Federal Reserve Board, *Prices in U. S. A. and Abroad*, Washington, 1924, pp. 2-4.

the Yokohama market. The depression was so sharp that in August of that year the highest price was only Y. 1,270,[1] or about 1/4 of the price 8 months before. After raw silk, the depression of cotton yarn next took place. The highest peak of cotton yarn was recorded in February 1920 with Y. 639.11 per bale (No. 20) in Osaka. But 3 months later, in May, this price went down to Y. 581.55, and one year later, Y. 263.07.[2] The result was a general depression for several years after March, 1920. Its effects were most disastrous, especially to manufacturing industries as shown by the above figures of diminution of capital.

3. UNFAVORABLE BALANCE OF PAYMENTS

With such high prices one can expect only an unfavorable balance of trade. So Japan began to tally each year an excess of imports, the figures of which may be seen below.

VISIBLE TRADE AFTER THE WAR

(million yen)

	Exports	Imports	Excess	4% Tech. Correction	Excess of Gold Imports	Trade Balance
1919	2,151	2,333	—179	93	—322	—408
1920	2,006	2,492	—486	99	—400	—787
1921	1,297	1,730	—433	69	—138	—502
1922	1,685	2,023	—337	80	— 1	—256
1923	1,497	2,119	—622	84	5	—533
						—2,486

The movement of this fall of commodity trade may be

[1] Department of Finance, *Kinyu Jikō*, 1924, p. 311. See also a chart prepared by The Silk Association of America, *Fifty-fifth Annual Report*, New York, 1927, p. 106.

[2] Department of Finance, *ibid.*, p. 312.

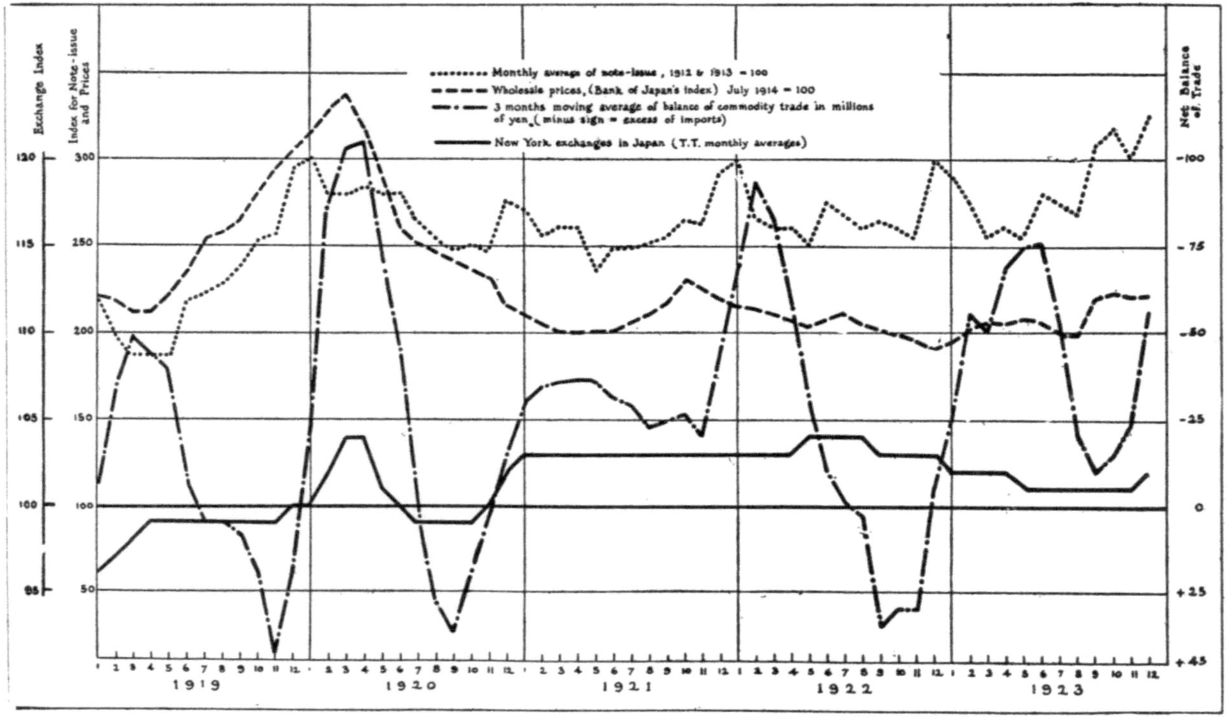

CHART V. PRICES, NOTES, TRADE AND EXCHANGES AFTER THE WAR

seen more vividly by the accompanying Chart V.[1] In this chart of monthly averages one will notice that the first influencing curve was the note circulation. The note circulation was then followed by the price curve and by trade and exchange movements. This can be illustrated in detail by elaborate trade statistics. But here let it suffice to show only the *general movement*. The higher the curves of notes and prices went, the larger became the *minus* quantity of trade; and so with exchanges.

The trade with U. S. A. began to be adverse because of high prices in Japan. For instance, raw silk which occupied more than 60 per cent of Japan's exports to the United States in 1920 was highest in price so that she not only exported less in quantity to America but also imported more goods from that country. Such was also the story of 1921 and 1919 in a less degree. In total, she had an excess of imports from America of 96 million yen during this period, while she had made 359 million yen excess of exports during the War. The trade with Australia was also unfavorable since Japan had imported from Australia an excess of 151 million yen during this period against 18 million yen excess of imports during the War. These differences were so great that the comparisons still remain valid even if we take the depreciation of money into consideration. Although trade with India and China was much disturbed by silver, boycotts and civil wars, yet in general, high prices at home were undoubtedly unfavorable to maintain the markets she opened during the War. The following summary of trade may be given for the period.

[1] In this chart, indices for monthly average of note issue and wholesale prices were calculated from the reports based on the Bank of Japan's *Economic Statistics of Japan*, 1925, pp. 5-7, pp. 111-12; and indices for exchange of New York were calculated from the reports of the Yokohama Specie Bank as shown in the Department of Finance's *Kinyu Jikō*, 1924, pp. 296-298. For exchange, the trend of the value of the dollar in Japan is shown. Notice in this chart as in others the seasonal trade fluctuations.

JAPAN'S COMMODITY TRADE ACCORDING TO COUNTRIES AFTER THE WAR[1]

(in millions of yen)

		Total exports of 5 years to	Total imports of 5 years from	Excess of exports or imports (—)
Asia	China	2,229	1,870	357
	India	588	1,482	—891
	Others	....	....	.....
	Total	3,826	4,225	—396
America	U. S. A.	3,226	3,320	—96
	Canada	....	....	.....
	Mexico	....	....	.....
	Chile and others	....	....	.....
	Total	3,335	3,441	—107
Europe and Australia	Europe	688	1,596	—909
	Australia	177	333	—151
	Others	....	....	.....
	Grand Total	8,639	10,697	—2,057

The movement of invisible trade was also like that of visible trade. There was a rapid and continuous decrease of our claims on foreign countries after 1919, a movement which was just the reverse of the boom war period. The chief causes of such a decline were the decrease in freight, charterage and insurance receipts, due to the resumption of maritime competition and the decrease in the government's receipts chiefly consisting of sales of munitions and interest on foreign loans, which may be seen in the following table.

[1] Figures are based on Department of Finance, *Kinyu Jikō Sankosho*, 1924, pp. 222-227.

Japan's Invisible Trade after the War[1]

(million yen)

	1919	1920	1921	1922	1923	Total
Receipts:						
I. Governmental:						
1. Sales of munitions, etc.	52.2	65.0	68.6	71.7	31.9	
II. Private:						
1. Freight and charterage	437.5	337.6	200.8	149.3	138.5	
2. Expenditures of foreign ships and companies in Japan	18.5	29.9	16.1	23.6	26.2	
3. Expenditures of foreigners in Japan	49.0	55.6	37.8	38.6	35.9	
4. Profits by Japanese abroad, immigrants' remittance and those carried home	131.8	126.1	110.8	106.3	112.0	
5. Profits and interest on foreign investments	59.7	50.5	46.0	28.7	28.0	
6. Insurance and premiums	101.2	105.8	82.2	76.6	75.6	
7. Others	65.1	60.7	..	5.1	12.6	
Total	915.0	837.2	562.3	479.9	460.7	3,255.1
Payments:						
I. Governmental:						
1. Interest on bonds	55.4	56.8	57.3	47.6	51.1	
2. Other payments	101.2	80.0	57.4	91.8	62.4	
II. Private:						
1. Expenditures of our ships abroad and of companies	74.7	100.5	76.8	61.9	60.1	
2. Expenditures of Japanese abroad	35.4	28.4	26.5	28.0	26.6	
3. Profits by foreigners in Japan	10.8	15.3	17.9	10.3	6.1	
4. Interest and profits of foreign investments	25.5	20.5	13.3	12.7	14.9	
5. Insurance and premiums	88.3	97.7	76.4	68.3	65.4	
6. Expenditures of Japanese enterprises abroad	2.6	3.6	3.0	4.0	3.6	
7. Others	16.7	13.6	37.9	.7	.7	
Total	410.6	416.4	366.5	325.3	290.9	1,809.7
Net Balance	504.4	420.8	195.8	154.6	169.8	1,445.4

Now if we add all these visible and invisible trade balances

[1] These figures are largely based on J. Inoue's *Japan's International Finance at Present and her Policy*, 1926, Tokio, Appendix vii.

together, we get a net trade deficit of 1,041 million yen for the period. For each year we have the following balances.

JAPAN'S NET BALANCE OF COMMERCE AFTER THE WAR

(million yen)

	1919	1920	1921	1922	1923	Total
Visible Trade Balance	—408	—787	—502	—256	—533	—2,486
Invisible Trade Balance.... ...	504	420	195	154	169	1,445
Net Trade Deficit	96	—367	—307	—102	—364	—1,041

Thus the relatively high prices in Japan causing unfavorable trade balances and the coming of foreign competition in ocean transportation caused Japan to lose 1,041 million yen during the period of 1919 to 1923.[1] Of this loss or deficit of 1,041 million yen, roughly 700 million yen were paid back out of specie holdings abroad, 400 million yen were paid out of bankers' funds of various forms kept abroad and of sales of domestic bonds and stocks, and the rest were freshly borrowed as in the case before the War. The following will show the details of such settlement.

[1] Of course, commercially this is not a loss but a deficit. It is simply meant that we paid more money in exchange of commodities and services. So far there is no change. This unfortunately ushered in a bad situation which will be discussed later.

CAPITAL MOVEMENT AFTER THE WAR [1]

(million yen)

	1919	1920	1921	1922	1923	Total
Credit:						
1. Net investment of foreigners in Japan *	17	..	..	..	123	....
2. Realizing of Japanese investments abroad by Japanese †	95	127	204	..	370	....
3. Decrease in exchange funds ‡	..	281	207	240	149	....
Total	112	408	411	240	642	1,810
Debit:						
1. Realizing of investments by foreigners *	..	41	104	25	82	....
2. Japanese investments abroad	208‡	..	..	113	196	....
Total	208	41	104	138	278	769
Net Credit Balance	—96	367	307	102	364	1,041

[1] The figures for 1919-1922 are based on the Department of Finance's *Kinyu Jikō*, Tokio, 1924, p. 26, and for those of 1923 are based on the Department of Finance's Quarterly Report of Finance and Economic Conditions of Japan, August, 1926, p. 26. Further explanations are cited below.

* The net investments of foreigners and those realized by them are calculated by the net increase or decrease of foreign investments in Japan as follows.

OUTSTANDING AMOUNTS OF FOREIGN INVESTMENTS IN JAPAN, 1919-1922

(million yen)

	Gov'nt foreign bonds	Domestic bonds sold out	Local gov't bonds	Debentures floated abroad	Foreigners investments in Japan	Total	Increase or decrease (—)
1919	1,311	63	147	165	35	1,721	17
1920	1,418	34	140	47	30	1,680	— 41
1921	1,362	18	130	33	25	1,576	—104
1922	1,358	5	134	26	25	1,550	— 25

† ‡. (See footnotes on next page).

Thus financially the period is characterized, first, by the heavy realization of Japanese investments abroad, and, second, by the heavy decrease in the exchange funds of both government and exchange bankers, and, third, by the beginning of sales of domestic bonds abroad again. In other words, this practically amounts to saying that that portion which Japan gained during the War and kept abroad was practically lost during this period. And in addition, domestic bonds were even exported as they yielded higher interest. And the rest of the war gain will be seen mainly in the increase of Japan's gold holding at home which was as follows.

INCREASE OF JAPAN'S GOLD HOLDING AT HOME[1]
(million yen)

	Total	Abroad	At home
At the end of 1913	376	246	130
" " 1923	1,652	444	1,208
Increase of gold at home	....	....	1,078

† These figures are deductively arrived at. But they roughly correspond to those estimated by J. Inoue. *Vide supra*, p. 64, footnote 1.

‡ The gold funds as called or more exactly exchange funds kept abroad by the government and the Bank of Japan were gradually decreased as they were sold out to exchange bankers as follows (million yen) (Department of Finance, *Kinyu Jikō*, Tokio, 1924, pp. 67-69).

	Gold funds	Increase or decrease (—)
At the end of 1918	1,135	.....
" " 1919	1,343	208
" " 1920	1,062	—281
" " 1921	855	—207
" " 1922	615	—240
" " 1923	444	—171

[1] Department of Finance, *Kinyu Jikō Sankosho*, Tokio, 1924, pp. 67-69.

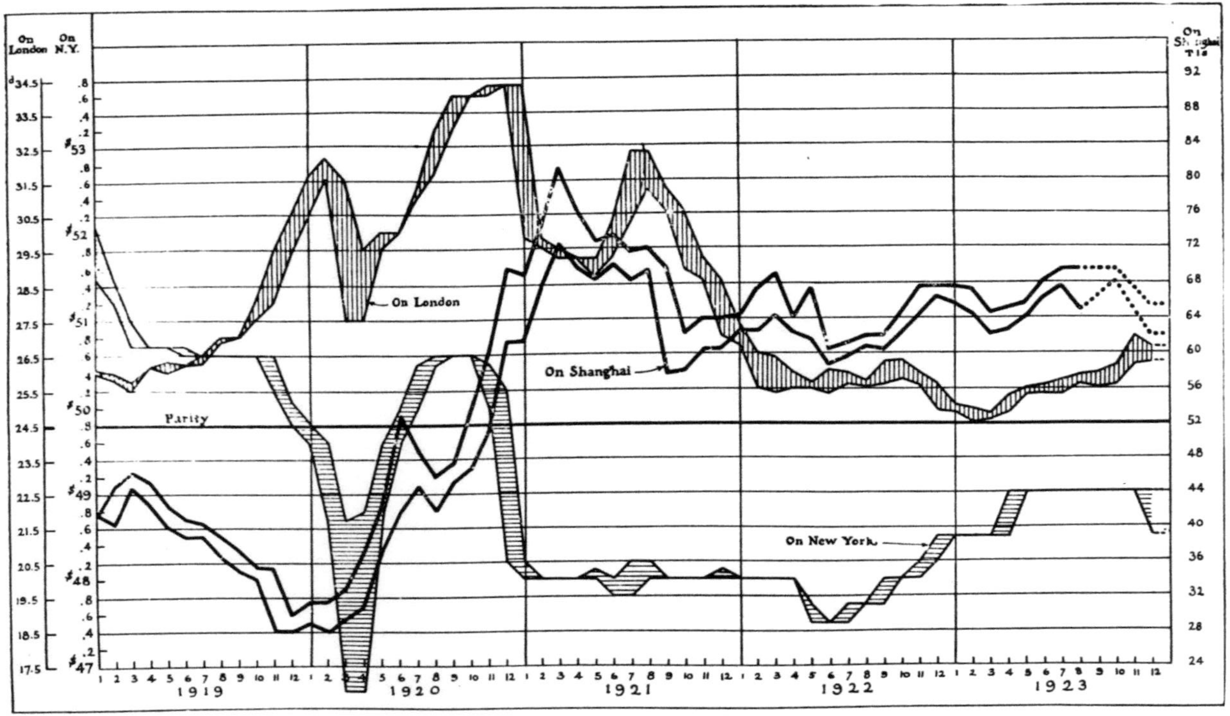

Chart VI. Exchanges on London, New York and Shanghai after the War

(Monthly high and low T. T. Rates)

Par on London *d.* 24.575 per ¥ 1.00

Par on New York $49.85 per ¥ 100.00

(Source: same as Chart II)

And the remaining five or six hundred million yen must have been distributed among her war-boomed industries. Thus if we summarize the financial account of Japan in relation to foreign countries during 1919 to 1923, we get the following statement.

BALANCE OF INTERNATIONAL PAYMENTS, 1919-1923

(million yen)

	1919	1920	1921	1922	1923
Credit:					
I. Net exports of gold and silver	..	..	..	1	5
II. Net invisible trade balance........	504	420	195	154	169
III. Foreign investments in Japan	17	..	..	..	123
Realizing of investments by Japanese	95	190	204	..	370
Decrease in exchange funds	..	218	207	240	149
Total	616	828	606	395	816
Debit:					
I. Net imports of merchandise	86	387	364	257	538
II. Net imports of gold and silver	322	400	138	..	..
III. Realizing of investments by foreigners	..	41	104	25	82
Japanese investments abroad......	208	..	..	113	196
Total	616	828	606	395	816

4. EXCHANGE MOVEMENTS

First of all, let us see the facts of the exchange movement. The accompanying Chart VI shows that between the London exchange and the New York exchange there was a wide divergence in the movement between this period and the war period.[1] This was due to the outside cause; namely, the

[1] *Cf.* Chart VI with Chart II, p. 69. The source of Chart VI is the same as Chart II.

fall of New York-London cross-rates. Inasmuch as Japan had now been concentrating foreign exchange funds in New York, the fall of the New York-London cross-rates simply meant to her that she ought to reduce exchange rates on London accordingly. The assertion that this passive movement of London exchange in Japan to the cross-rates after March, 1919 is conclusively established in the accompanying Chart VII,[1] although the former was more sensitive than the latter and fluctuated behind the latter. In other words, in Japan the movement of dollar exchange was like that of wholesale prices, while the movement of London exchange was like that of retail prices.

Since London exchanges in Japan had to follow dollar exchanges, all other European exchanges (and in a less degree Oriental exchanges) such as mark and franc exchanges had, of course, to follow dollar exchanges. Thus, for instance, the great collapse of marks during 1919-1924 and of franc during 1919 to date[2] occurred simultaneously in Japan. Before the War the yen was about 2 marks (par being 2.0924 marks). But this dropped to 15 marks in January, 1919, and to 27 marks in December, 1919. This was further collapsed to 2,705 marks in December, 1922 and to 3,010,000 marks in August, 1923. But since the adoption on the part of Germany of the Rentenmark (1 Rentenmark=1,000,000,000,000 paper marks) in October, 1923 and other subsequent measures such as the establishment of the Gold Discount Bank, the reorganization of the Reichsbank in October, 1924 along

[1] The sources of this chart relating to Japan-London exchanges are found in the Yokohama Specie Bank's Weekly, while those relating to New York-London exchanges in James W. Angell's *The Theory of International Prices*, Cambridge, 1926, pp. 530-531.

[2] U. S. Senate Commission of Gold and Silver Inquiry, Foreign Currency and Exchange Investigation, Series 9, Washington, 1925, vol. i, pp. 325-332, 411-417.

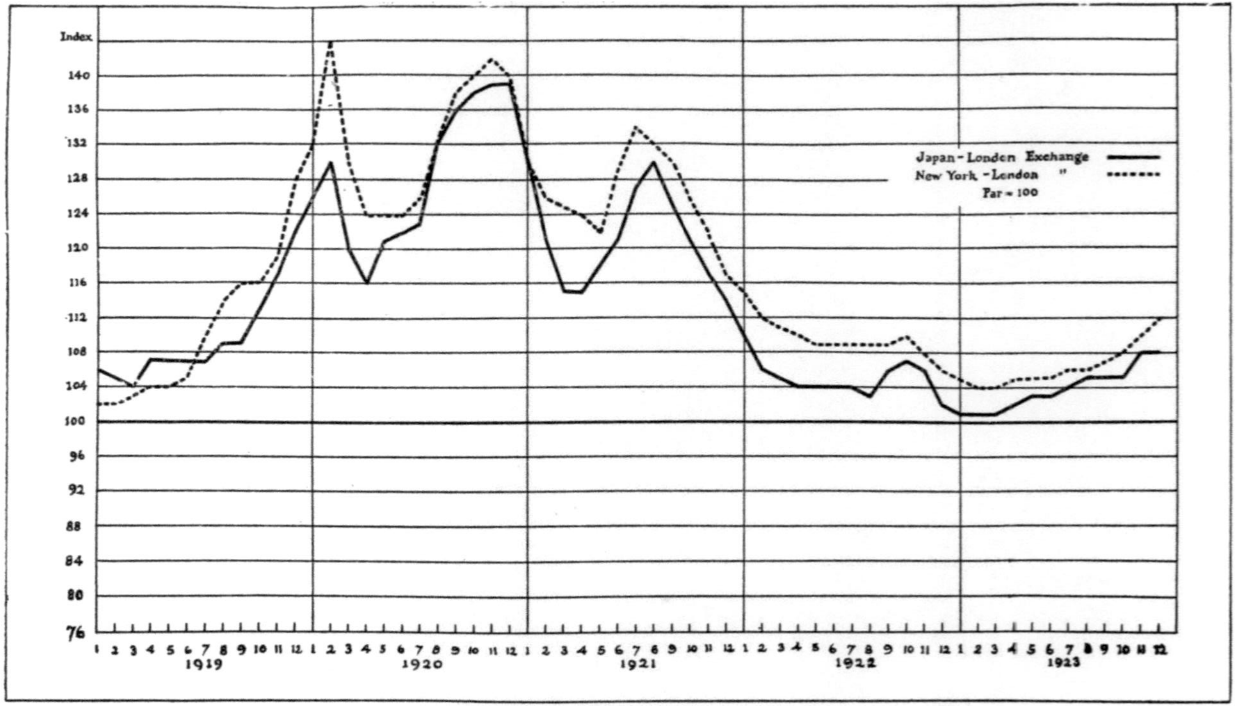

CHART VII. JAPAN-LONDON AND NEW YORK-LONDON EXCHANGES AFTER THE WAR

(Monthly average of T. T. Rates)

.... the dollar's premium on the sterling

———— the yen's premium on the sterling

the line of the Dawes plan, and the general stabilization policy, the new mark exchange has been quite stable. The fluctuations as indicated in mark quotation in Japan after November, 1923 were largely due to the fluctuations of yen exchange and not to the mark exchange. This point can be well illustrated by the correlation of the fluctuations of Japan-New York exchanges and Japan-Hamburg exchanges. The dominance of New York exchange over all other exchanges in Japan can be also shown in the case of French exchange and its collapse. Before the War the yen was about 2.5 francs (par being 2.583). But this dropped to an average of 12 francs in 1924, to 13.5 francs in 1925, and to 17 francs at the end of 1926. These slumps in Japan are in complete harmony with the record shown in the New York exchange market on France, for in Japan exchanges on European centers during this period were largely fixed according to the dollar exchanges on these centers.

The great fall of New York-London cross-rates in the post-war period has been attributed to many causes, differing sometimes completely from one another according to different writers. T. E. Gregory [1] and others seem to hold that inflation was the chief cause; and "to complain of the effects of speculation . . . is to put the cart before the horse". But on the other hand, James W. Angell and others hold the opposite view. According to the latter, speculation first affected the exchanges; exchanges pushed prices up, and last of all the note circulation.[2] Whatever the case may be, it is the fact that the exchange began to fall when England ceased to control exchanges through J. P. Morgan and Company in March 20, 1919 and after the termination of the general

[1] T. E. Gregory, *Foreign Exchange*, Oxford, 1922, pp. 80-90; *The Return to Gold*, London, 1925, pp. 30-31.

[2] James W. Angell, *ibid.*, pp. 426-439.

Inter-Allied arrangements. The effect of this fall was soon reflected in the Japan-London exchange. This is why during 1919 and up to February, 1920, the London exchange in Japan was moving in the opposite direction to that of the dollar exchange. And this is why the gap between the London exchange and the New York exchange became widened since 1920 and why the London exchange fluctuated so violently. In the case of the sterling exchange in Japan, then, the causes of its fluctuations during the post-war period are largely found in the fluctuations of New York-London exchange, and are neither directly traceable to the Japan-London balance of payments nor to their relative prices, for a larger volume of international payments was then effected through New York as the dollar became the standard exchange in Japan. Moreover, the price movement between the two countries, Japan and Great Britain, was nearly on the same trend during this period.

In the case of fluctuations in the American exchange in Japan, the case is different. Here we find direct causal relations in the monetary, trade, and financial situations between the two countries. So it is here best to divide the period into the following sub-periods and see the different turns of events connected with exchanges.

(1) Fall of exchange in 1919 up to March, 1920.

(2) Sudden rise and fall of exchange in 1920.

(3) Relatively stabilized exchange during 1921 to 1923.

(1) The early fall of yen exchange on America in 1919 was, of course, due to the expectation of free gold movements in America and actual abandonments of restrictions on silver in April and on gold in June, 1919. But the later and more rapid fall of yen exchange on America during October, 1919 to March, 1920 was due to the abnormally rapid rise of prices in Japan caused by the aforesaid credit expansion,

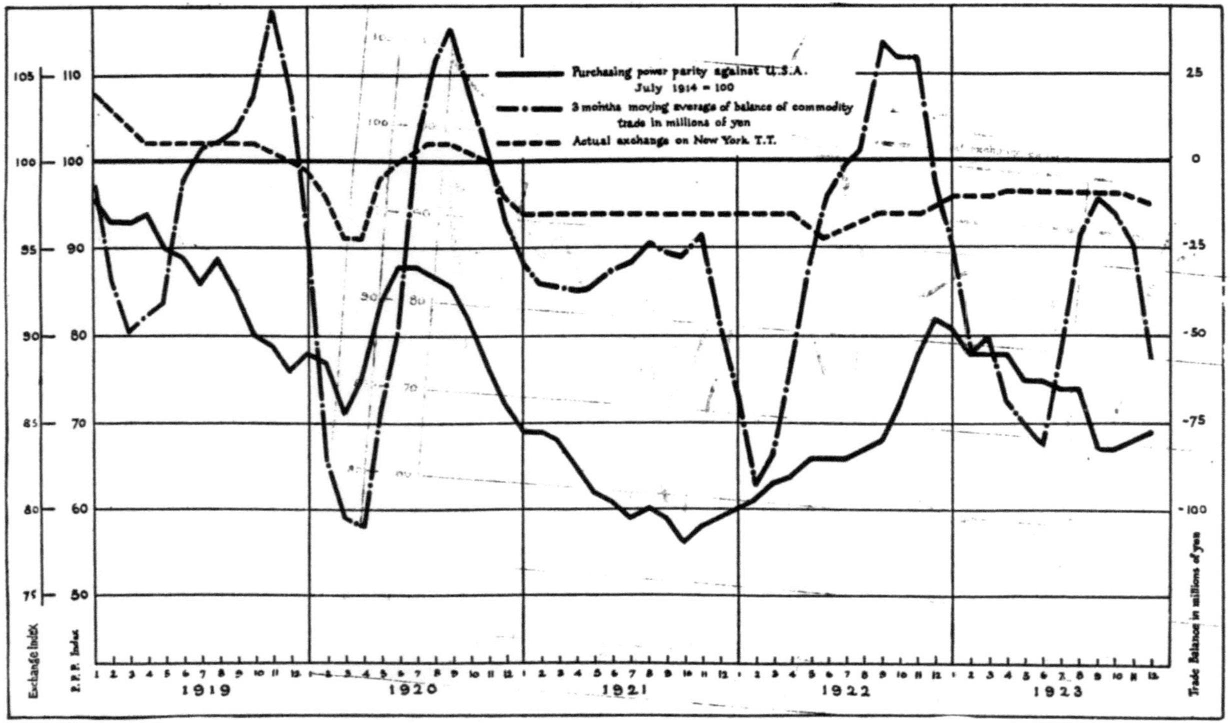

CHART VIII. PURCHASING POWER PARITY, BALANCE OF TRADE AND ACTUAL EXCHANGES AFTER THE WAR

inviting a sudden and the largest excess of imports for the period.

(2) But when notes were contracting and bank credits were liquidating as previously illustrated, prices declined even more sharply, causing a little improvement in trade. This was aided by Finance Minister Wakatsuki's wholesale selling of gold funds mostly kept in New York. Such selling amounted to roughly 281 million yen. This had, of course, practically the same effect as the free movement of specie, and quickly restored the exchange. And by speculation it even went up 1 per cent above par, but when prices again began to rise and the discrepancy between the Japanese and American prices increased, the exchange again dropped 3 per cent below par. All this was occurred in 1920, the most eventful and unadjusted and panicky year after the War.

(3) When the exchange dropped 3 per cent, it was virtually stabilized at that level during 1921 and 1922. But when the gradual fall of Japanese prices and the gradual rise of American prices had approached each other more closely at the end of 1922, the exchange began to recover a little more. And the year 1923 saw another upward price movement; and when this was augmented by the great Earthquake in September, the trade remained unfavorable throughout the year even during the months of the usual exporting season. But the exchange was virtually stabilized at around $48.50 by draining gold funds, realizing of Japanese investments abroad and by exporting domestic bonds as mentioned before.

Thus in general we are convinced by the statistical analysis that the first movement in this period was the relative prices of the two countries as represented in the purchasing power parity curves in the accompanying Chart VIII; and this was then followed by the movement of trade and lastly by exchanges.[1] It was true that in the case of the panic of 1920 speculation had helped to widen the fluctuation of exchange, but that was all. Exchange never could be the cause of the movements of prices and trade generally for any long period of time. Our statistical analysis as presented in Chart VIII clearly disproves such a statement of sequence. On the other hand, the purchasing power parity theory cannot also adequately explain the exchange movement of this period except in a very general sort of way; for first, although there was a kind of correlation between the purchasing power parity and the actual exchange during the first two years, yet the gaps between the two curves were too great, while second, for the rest of the three years there was no sort of correlation.[2]

A few words may be said about silver exchanges for the period. The continuous rise of silver since the latter part of 1914 kept up throughout the War and continued until December, 1919 when the price of silver in New York hit the highest mark at $1.375 per ounce.[3] Then, in 1920 it began

[1] *See* accompanying Chart VIII. In this chart, indices for exchange rates are calculated from the reports of the Yokohama Specie Bank, while price indices are based on the Bank of Japan's reports. The Chart is again to show the general movements of purchasing power parities, balance of trade and exchanges.

[2] The gap was too wide in 1921 to entertain the purchasing power parity theory. The element of pegging has been too great. *See* Chart VII, p. 120.

[3] The cause of high price in silver in the latter part of the War and in 1919 was the absorption of silver in India and China. Regarding it, U. S. Federal Reserve *Bulletin* reports as follows (Federal Reserve *Bulletin*, August, 1921, p. 938): "It was China that caused such an insistent demand for silver in 1919, heightened perhaps by speculators, as to drive the price to its peak in January, 1920. But by that time the demand was fairly satisfied."

"By the summer of 1919 the Indian demand for silver ceased."

Also *cf.* Cross, Ira B.: *Domestic and Foreign Exchange*, New York, 1923, p. 443, Chart VIII.

The world's production of silver during this period increased over the war period by 65 million ounces.

tc decline rapidly until March, 1921 when the lowest point was reached at *c.* 52.75. After that and during the rest of the three years, the trend of silver fluctuated around *c.* 65.[1] Now the exchange on Shanghai in Japan took precisely the same course.[2] It was continuously falling up to December 1919, then a sudden rise took place during 1920, and for the rest of the period it remainded around 64 taels per Y. 100. Such a course was natural, for as was already explained in Chapter III, exchanges on Shanghai in Japan have been primarily based on silver quotations in New York and London, and inasmuch as these quotations are either quoted in dollars or sterling, weak yen exchanges on New York and London have been the next controlling factor. So although trade with China for this period saw a successive decrease in Japan's excess of exports,[3] yet this factor had less to do with the general movement of exchange on China. But the only exception was the direct shipment of silver to China in 1923 to the amount of 5 million yen,[4] the object of which was to partly pay for the trade deficit and to partly guard against undue speculation in Shanghai.

[1] *Cf.* George E. Eddins' "International Silver Market," *Commerce Monthly*, Oct., 1926, p. 5.

[2] *See* the trend of exchanges on Shanghai in Chart VI, p. 119.

[3] Japan's excess of commodity exports to China for this period was as follows: (mil. yen)

	Exports	Imports	Excess	Total
1919	597	487	112	
1920	523	414	109	
1921	364	303	61	357
1922	405	316	88	
1923	340	353	—13	

[4] In ordinary years, silver movement between the two countries is inflow or outflow of two to three million yen per year.

The same thing can be said about the rupee exchange except that since 1922 the rupee was greatly helped by the improvement shown in the London exchange. In the early part of 1919, 100 yen could buy 147 rupees, but in February, 1920 when silver went up to 89.50 pence per ounce in London, the same 100 yen could now buy only 96.5 rupees. And then the rupee rapidly went down, and in March, 1921 it reached as low as 30.625 pence per ounce and, consequently, the exchange was raised as much as Rs. 193.5 in Japan. This great fall of silver was mainly accounted for by the great fall of prices in general, the recovery of rates, followed by a corresponding recovery of exchange on London in Japan and a greater production of silver after 1921,[1] while in China and India the absorption of silver became less than that of the war period.

But since the latter part of 1921 when the London exchange began to improve rapidly and consequently when the condition of the Indian currency was improving, her exchange was rapidly reaching the pre-war basis. Added to this, the Indian trade with Japan remained much more favorable to India than the war period, as the following figures show.

[1] The great production of silver after 1921 was mainly due to the greater production in Mexico.

WORLD'S PRODUCTION OF SILVER AFTER THE WAR
(millions of ounces)

	Total	Mexico	U. S. A.	Canada
1919	182	66	57	16
1920	173	67	55	13
1921	172	64	53	14
1922	211	81	56	19
1923	240	91	66	19
1924	239	91	64	20
1925	242	93	61	20

	Price of silver in London pence per ounce			Exchange on Bombey Rs. per Y100			Exchange on London pence per Y1.00		
	high	low	average	high	low	average	high	low	average
1919..	79.125	47.75	57.01	147	106.5	130	30.5	25.6	27.
1920..	98.5	38.86	61.56	208.5	96.5	138.5	34.4	27.5	31.5
1921..	43.37	30.61	36.81	211	167.5	185.5	52.5	27.1	29.9
1922..	37.37	30.37	34.43	172.5	157	166.3	27.5	24.9	25.9
1923..	33.68	30.5	31.99	162.2	145.7	155.8	27.	24.6	25.5

TRADE WITH INDIA AFTER THE WAR
(million yen)

	Japan's excess of imports from India		Exports	Imports	Excess of imports
1914..........	—134	1919..........	116	319	—202
1915	—105	1920..........	192	394	—202
1916..........	—107	1821..........	84	210	—125
1917..........	—122	1922..........	97	254	—156
1918..........	— 65	1923	99	305	—206
	—533				—891

5. FAILURE OF EXCHANGE POLICY

Having discussed the economic side of the exchange situation in Japan, we are now prepared to discuss the political side of the exchange problem.

When the War stopped in November, 1918, Japanese exchange bankers were not immediately relieved, as their funds were still accumulated in New York and could not be removed profitably, while at home they were short of funds to finance exports. So in May, 1919 the Bank of Japan headed by Governor J. Inoue, introduced the use of bank acceptances for import yen bills and the "Bank of Japan's stamped bill" for export bills.[1] The use of the former was not

[1] J. Inoue, *ibid.*, pp. 67-77.

altogether new. Its use had been greatly encouraged and favored by the government authorities. But due to a limited amount of yen bills, its effect was very much limited. The latter was new. A "stamped bill" was nothing but a finance bill drawn by the exchange banker and stamped by the Bank of Japan on the understanding that such finance bill should always originate from the drawing banker's buying of a real export bill and that its amount was never to exceed the original export bill and its maturity not to exceed more than 90 days. But this new device was never developed to any great extent, and in a few years they practically disappeared, for there were neither discount markets nor even discount houses; besides the Japanese are not accustomed to the "open" market business. Therefore, they could not take advantage of the discount market.[1]

Meanwhile, America lifted her embargo on gold in June, 1919, and because of the high rates of yen exchange at this time, gold was flowing to Japan quite heavily. In 1919, 1920, and 1921 net gold imports were 322, 400, and 138 million yen respectively. However, the successive heavy imports of gold not only helped inflation and high prices at home but also reaped a situation where, because of relatively high prices, exports became almost impossible. In 1920 alone they saw the excess of imports at 486 million yen, and in 1921 even more. The exchange was naturally lowered. And as the exchange market was crowded with these import bills, the problem of exchange bankers was how to pay off these debit bills. And since export bills could not counterbalance more voluminous import bills, bankers' own ex-

[1] G. Odate speaks as if there was an acceptance market developed in Japan at this time; and devotes one full period to this discussion. But this is merely an erroneous interpretation of stamped bills. *See* G. Odate, *Japan's Financial Relations with the United States*, New York, 1922, pp. 71-77.

change funds were first utilized; and when these were exhausted, they began to buy funds held abroad by the Bank of Japan and the government. The government was willing to do this in order to peg the lowering exchanges. Thus the exchange bankers' funds were first exhausted, and then the funds of the government and the Bank of Japan were next heavily exhausted.[1]

Although there was, during the War-Cabinets of Okuma and Terauchi, a government policy of maintaining favorable rates of exchange for the exporters' sake, yet there was no direct exchange control. Gold was left free. And the exchange rates were only a little above par. But when the government under the Hara cabinet with K. Takahashi as Finance Minister followed the American fashion and put an embargo on gold and silver[2] in September, 1917, the era of

[1] Since 1920 the records were as follows:

JAPAN'S GOLD FUNDS HELD ABROAD AFTER 1920

(million yen)

End of Month	1920	1921	1922	1923
1	1,321	1,046	814	607
2	1,232	1,017	758	597
3	1,187	996	700	595
4	1,180	976	676	596
5	1,178	958	665	593
6	1,163	947	647	589
7	1,158	930	637	576
8	1,158	922	637	575
9	1,151	915	621	559
10	1,122	907	621	565
11	1,071	877	620	512
12	1,062	855	615	444

Notice the rapid decrease of funds abroad.

[2] Both exporting and melting were prohibited by the decree of the Department of Finance, Decree No. 26 and No. 28.

direct governmental pegging began to follow and the responsibility of the government in matters of exchange was firmly established. Of course, the object of this embargo was to safeguard and keep the specie within the country. But unfortunately this was not only futile but also harmful to finance trade and to keep prices down. It was futile, because the War was waged in Europe. Japan had nothing to do in Europe but to expand her industries at home and trade abroad. Moveover, since the participation of America in the War, the victory for the Allies was simply a matter of time. It was harmful to the trade, because there became no means to pay for the Indian cotton we so badly needed; besides it raised exchange rates. The government was too superstitious in protecting gold, as if gold were the sole source of credit and value.

In June, 1919, the United States lifted the embargo on gold, but Japan did not follow suit. Herein lies Japan's second error. For after the Armistice and especially after the American lifting of the embargo, there was nothing to fear. In July, 1919, Japan had 1,701 million yen gold; (463 million yen at home and 1,238 million yen abroad), or 4 times more at home and 6 times more abroad than the year preceding the War. And as the note issue in the latter half of 1919 was rapidly increasing, prices were correspondingly enhanced. Now the cry for free movement of gold was started both at Parliament and in public. But Finance Minister Takahashi coldly replied by saying that the enhancement of prices was due to the world-wide movement. But this was only a partial truth. What Japan should have cared for was not a mere rising movement of prices but *relatively* higher price movement. But the Finance Minister failed to see the point. In his opinion an average note issue of 1,200 million yen at the end of 1919 absolutely needed more gold at home, and he kept on increasing it [1] without releasing it to flow out and to better finance trade and restore exchange, and first of all, to reduce the level of prices. Instead, he stuck to his policy and invited a great inflation, as pictured in Chart V (page 113) and caused virtually the abandonment of the gold standard.[2] Even as late as in January, 1922, the same Finance Minister Takahashi, then Premier as well, either mockingly or ignorantly replied in the Parliament to the effect that "the standstill of our

[1] The volumes of gold holdings at home were as follows:

INCREASE IN THE STOCK OF GOLD AT HOME, 1919-1923
(million yen)

End of month	1919	1920	1921	1922	1923
1	449	694	1,137	1,224	1,213
2	448	691	1,153	1,221	1,211
3	446	684	1,164	1,220	1,208
4	445	680	1,188	1,222	1,206
5	445	693	1,201	1,223	1,204
6	443	749	1,208	1,221	1,204
7	463	782	1,217	1,218	1,204
8	488	825	1,223	1,218	1,204
9	526	876	1,222	1,220	1,210
10	545	937	1,225	1,220	1,213
11	616	1,017	1,227	1,217	1,211
12	702	1,116	1,225	1,215	1,208

Notice the rapid increase of gold at home.

[2] Strictly speaking, the gold standard has been kept in Japan even after the gold embargo of September, 1917, as the conversion of notes is nominally unlimited. But practically speaking, the conversion was only possible for certain persons for certain purposes such as for dentists, for dental purposes in which case the government through the Yokohama Specie Bank was selling not gold coins but gold bullion at Y 5.02 per 2 *fun* of pure gold. And the people were buying increasingly, and smuggling was going on. So the government on Nov. 3, 1924, passed an ordinance promulgating that thereafter the selling of bullion was to be fixed at the current rate of exchange. However, inflation took place in Japan not right after the embargo in 1917 but gradually after 1918 and greatly after 1919. Thus, Japan, in reality, became a paper standard country.

exports was mainly due to the lack of purchasing power of the foreign countries." Now such a reply was simply to ignore the facts. We have already learned that our price level was moving far above that of the United States since 1919 and even above Great Britain since 1921. That the sequence of events was first note issue, then unfavorable trade,[1] then unfavorable exchange can be well illustrated in Chart V and Chart VIII (page 123).

Thus Finance Minister Takahashi in his administration of almost 4 years, September 1918–June 1922, not only missed ample chances of lifting gold embargo, but also completely failed to readjust prices after the War, and virtually led Japan into the paper standard. The strengthening of gold reserve after the War without the actual redemption and free movement of gold was neither a guaranty against inflation nor an antiseptic against a national monetary corruption.

The blame, however, should not be borne by one Finance Minister but by his political party, the Seiyu-kai. For the Seiyu-kai always stood for " positive policy " which meant to encourage industries and trade by extending credits, floating-loans, and by passing various governmental measures of all sorts and undertakings. One natural result of such a policy was to swell the state expenditures thereby to exhance prices as already mentioned.

Thus, when Japan needed an economic readjustment and deflation more than anything else after the War, what she got was the Seiyu-kai's " positive policy " which caused high prices, excess of imports, unfavorable exchanges, and finally exhaustion of gold funds abroad, as they began to peg exchanges in the early parts of 1921 and 1922 by selling gold funds abroad at the government's desired rates of exchange.

[1] *See* Chart IV, p. 110.

It is thus known that the government's artificial pegging was an utter failure.[1]

When the Takahashi cabinet was replaced by T. Kato's cabinet in June, 1922, Mr. Ichiki was appointed as Finance Minister. He immediately announced his famous " 19 means of adjusting prices " and later in September the exclusion of gold funds held abroad for note-issuing purposes. Such measures coupled with the upward trend of the American prices helped the Japanese exports. And this was why the excess of imports for 1922 was smaller when compared to that of the year preceding or following. But on the whole Finance Minister Ichiki never touched the real sore-spot of the credit control. For he still increased the national expenditures of 1923 and the amount of domestic loans which gave occasions for another note expansion and the upward trend of prices since the latter part of 1922 and throughout 1923. However, relatively high rates of exchange at this time were largely due to the government's pegging at the expense of gold funds abroad.[2] Then, the great earthquake of September 1, 1923 came. T. Kato's cabinet was replaced by the Yamamoto earthquake-cabinet with J. Inoue as Finance Minister. Japan at that time had only 575 million yen worth of gold funds abroad, although at home she still held 1,210 million yen gold.[3] But in the eyes of Mr. Inoue this much gold was absolutely needed in Japan against an outstanding sum of 1,287 million yen notes. Moreover, he was printing more notes in order to meet a great emergency arising out of the earthquake. So he would neither lift the gold embargo nor pursue the policy of his pre-

[1] *Cf.* J. Inoue, *Japan's Economic and Financial Situations after the War*, Tokio, 1925, pp. 116-117, *passim.*

[2] *Vide supra*, p. 129.

[3] All these figures represent the outstanding amounts on the day just before the Earthquake, August 31, 1923.

decessors by selling gold funds abroad. The result was again obvious. At home inflation was still going on; and abroad the beginning of that great exchange speculation of 1924 and 1925 was started first slowly in October and more vigorously in Nevember and December 1923, inviting a great exchange slump. And thus the government exchange policy for the period ended in a complete failure.

6. SUMMARY

From the foregoing we have seen that the post-war period of 1919-1923 was economically just the reverse of the war period of 1914-1918. Prices were high, and both visible and invisible trade were unfavorable to Japan. The fund abroad was fast decreasing. From the accountant's point of view, nearly one-half of what Japan gained during the War was lost during this period.

It was during this period that the prestige of the sterling exchange was definitely lost and the dollar exchange was established as the standard exchange, and consequently the method of exchange operation was wholly changed.

The sequence of events was, in the main, the reverse of the preceding period; namely, first the expansion of credit, followed by high prices, and then excess of imports, unfavorable balance of payments, and finally, falling exchanges. But the reason why relatively high rates of exchange were actually maintained was because the exchange was pegged at the expense of gold funds held abroad.

The means of financing foreign trade were still inadequate. Acceptances and "stamped bills" were introduced. But without an enactment of bank laws, without preparations for new methods and adequate discount markets, such an introduction was simply a one-sided arrangement between the central bank and the individual bankers concerned; besides it was altogether sporadic in that it would disappear with the resignation of a certain Finance Minister or the Governor of the Bank of Japan. So it was natural that, in the course of a few years, the so-called stamped bills were totally lost to sight.

The government's exchange policy was unfortunately erroneous. Its gold embargo was not only futile but also left many evils behind to readjust the price situation. The government had lost ample chances to lift the embargo when Japan could easily and harmlessly do so as there was yet plenty of gold funds abroad and exchanges had not yet slumped. On the contrary, the false policy of the government ushered Japan into what was virtually a paper standard régime. "As the result of such mistaken policies, the country was now suffering from high cost of production, unfavorable balance of trade, increase of unemployment, and other symtoms regrettable from the economic and social standpoint." [1]

[1] Dr. J. Soyoda, "Economic Situation in Japan," *Economic Journal,* June, 1923, p. 252.

CHAPTER V

Yen Exchange and the Balance of Payments After the Great Earthquake, 1924-1927

I. REAL ECONOMIC EFFECTS OF THE GREAT EARTHQUAKE

The earthquake of September 1, 1923 cost Japan 70,000 deaths, 300,000 wounded and the loss of 7 billion yen[1] or three times the cost to Japan of the Russo-Japanese war. This loss of 7 billion yen represents the total destruction of Yokohama, and ¾ destruction of Tokio, as well as of their vicinities. Nearly all public utilities, buildings, houses, bridges and everything else went to pieces and burned. On September 2, amid continued burning and quaking the Yamamoto cabinet was formed, which immediately promulgated various protective and relief measures such as an emergency confiscation ordinance, martial law, excess profits law, moratorium, exemption and reduction of taxes and of customs duties, establishment of the Tokio Recovery Council, the regulation of supply of commodities, and the government's guaranty for rediscounting earthquake bills by the Bank of Japan up to the limit of 100 million yen.

Meanwhile, the people began to rehabilitate the city, and by September 19, 252 banks in Tokio had reopened for business. The Tokio Bill Clearance House had cleared over 159 million yen by the end of the month, 1,460 million yen by the end of October, and 2,003 million yen by the end of November, and so on, while Yokohama's recovery was somewhat slower.

[1] The loss has been reported variously from 5 to 10 billion yen as they were calculated under different capitalization methods. The most conservative figure arrived at by the Economic Research Department of the Osaka Mainichi Shimbun was 7 billion yen. The *Mainichi Almanac for 1924*, Osaka, 1924, pp. 209-233.

Its clearing house cleared 8 million yen in October, 50 million yen in November, and so on.

The economic effects of the earthquake were; *A. fiscally,* (1) decrease in the government revenue,[1] (2) many government enterprises and undertakings which were authorized by the preceding Diet were postponed; *B. financially,* (1) over 432 million yen of bills were outstanding waiting to be rediscounted by the Bank of Japan, (2) as the result of various rehabilitation measures, advances of the Central bank increased with a rapid expansion of note issues. At the end of December 1923, the amount of such issue reached the highest peak in the history of Japan's finance so far with 1,703 million yen. (3) Prices were temporaily raised up to December, 1923, but thereafter they declined, although yen exchange began to drop fearfully after October, 1923, reaching the lowest point in October, 1924 with 24 per cent below par. Speculation was wild. *C. Industrially,* however, export manufacturing was less harmed than some of the domestic industries. But in general, as Tokio and Yokohama have not been the manufacturing centres as Osaka and Nagoya are, the productive capacity of Japan, especially in relation to foreign countries, should not be considered greatly injured. From the nation's industrial point of view, the depression of 1920-21 was even more harmful than the earthquake. *D. Commercially,* (1) exports were, of course, curtailed because of less goods and relatively higher prices, (2) on the other hand, imports were suddenly increased primarily because of the great demand for reconstruction materials.

On the whole, however, financial loss was most injurious to the economic readjustment in the post-earthquake period, for at home the so-called unpaid earthquake bills were hanging in the air, and abroad the yen suffered from the loss of

[1] The government spent 66 million yen of Surplus of the preceding year; besides 40 million yen in taxes, and 30 million yen in customs duties were reduced from the government's income.

confidence and value; consequently, Japan had to pay relatively more for obligations and received relatively less for claims.

2. GREAT EXCHANGE SLUMPS OF 1924, AND RAPID RECOVERY DURING 1925-27

We have already seen that since 1916 the New York exchange has been controlling factor in all other exchanges in Japan due to the ascendancy of New York's exchange and specie markets. But with the recovery of London exchange and her discount market, especially after the latter part of 1924 and finally the restoration of the gold standard in April 28, 1925,[1] exchange centres have come to be two instead of one. Consequently, the exchange operation in Japan as elsewhere began to look for New York- London cross-rates as the basis of all exchanges. In other words, New York-London exchanges have come to be wholesale prices, while all other exchanges have become retail prices. Retail prices must necessarily have to follow, in the main, wholesale prices. So in Japan, the London exchange has lately come to be more important than during the War and the post-war period. Yet New York's exchange by reason of America's sound monetary system and her surplus financial power still retains the position of being the standard of exchanges in Japan. Therefore, the external value of yen is yet best expressed in terms of dollars.

Now dollar exchanges in Japan after the War and up to the earthquake of September, 1923 had been largely pegged and maintained relatively at higher levels through the selling of gold exchange funds kept abroad by the government and the Bank of Japan. But at the time when the earthquake took place, these funds were heavily drained and therefore

[1] *Cf.* "The restoration of the gold standard in Great Britain" in *Political Science Quarterly*, March, 1926, pp. 35-7; Federal Reserve *Bulletin*, June, 1925.

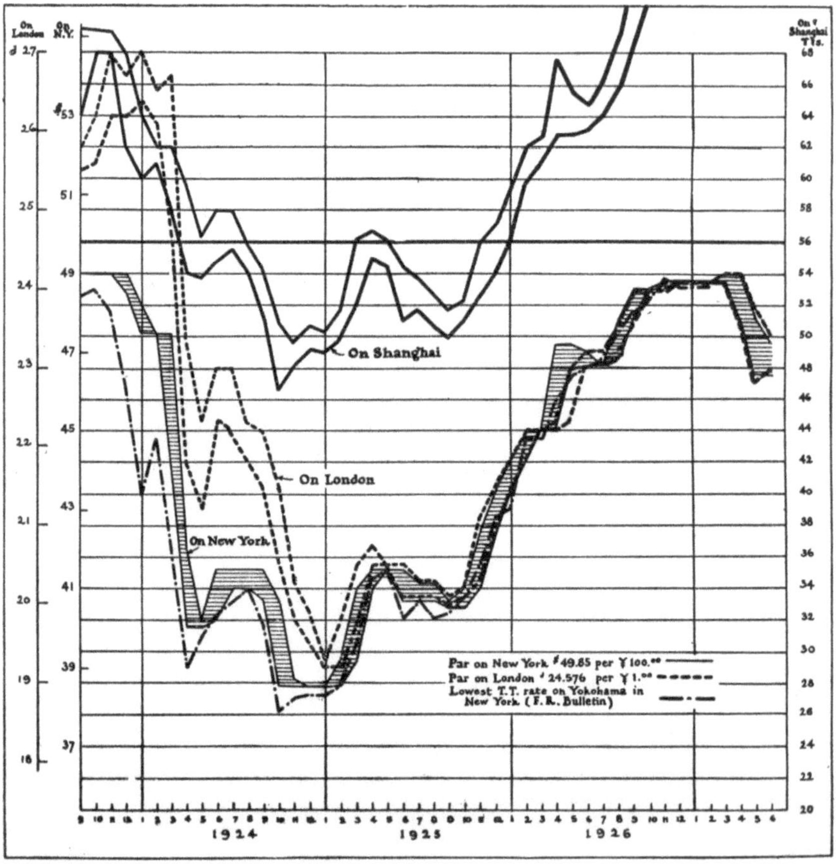

CHART IX. EXCHANGES ON LONDON, NEW YORK AND SHANGHAI AFTER THE GREAT EARTHQUAKE

(Monthly high and low T. T. Rates)

Par on London *d.* 24.575 per Y 1.00

Par on New York $49.85 per Y 100.00

(Source: same as Chart II)

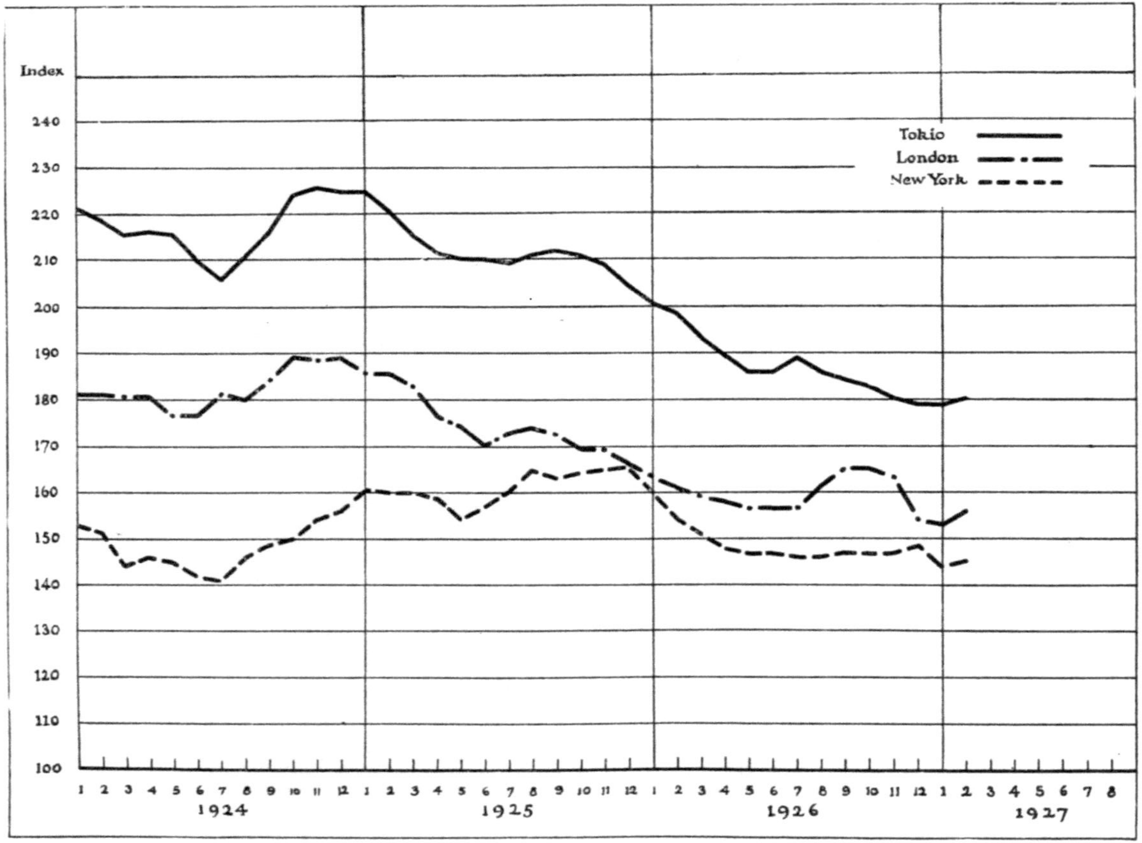

CHART X. TOKIO, LONDON AND NEW YORK WHOLESALE PRICES AFTER THE GREAT EARTHQUAKE
(July 1914 = 100)
(Source: same as Chart I)

were meagre after the successive excess of commodity imports. Foreigners were apt to take the volume of these funds as the barometer of Japan's prosperity and productivity. Then, the earthquake came. A great devastation of Japan was reported. Exchange speculators in New York, followed by those in London, Shanghai, and elsewhere, began to flood the markets with yen exchanges. The result was a 4 per cent slump in November, and a slump of 6½ per cent in December of that same year. Yet the government could not do much toward pegging as it had done before, as there were only 444 million yen left in gold holdings abroad. On the other hand, speculation was intensified when the ineffectiveness of the government's pegging became known. Already in January, 1924, the yen exchange in New York dropped 12 per cent. The government sold 152 million yen of gold funds abroad during January and February. This restored the rate 2 per cent in February, but in March the gold funds decreased to only 292 million yen, and speculation aided another drop of 6 per cent, and from April to August 4 per cent was restored chiefly due to the increase in Japan's exports. But when imports began to be greater in September, another exchange drop of 2 per cent was recorded, and in October, aided by speculation, a drop of 5 per cent took place in New York, making a total slump of 24 per cent below par, or $37.90 per Y. 100.00.[1] Such a drop was never before experienced in Japan, yet the government was simply helpless to do anything. Bankers, business men and economists were once more divided in their opinions as to whether the lifting of the gold embargo would restore the exchange.

Fortunately, however, after December, 1924, Japanese prices were declining.[2] This was chiefly due to Finance Min-

[1] *See* Chart IX. The dotted line represents the lowest T. T. rates on Yokohama in New York. Source: *Yokohama Specie Bank Weekly.*

[2] *See* accompanying Chart X. Source: Bank of Japan, *Economic Statistics of Japan*, Tokio, 1925.

ister Hamaguchi's policy of retrenchment and actual shipments of gold to America in order to stabilize and finally restore exchanges. Relatively lower prices aided exports; and the exchange steadily improved after February, 1925, and by the end of that year 8 per cent was restored. After January, 1926, the restoration was even more rapid, recording an 11 percent recovery, making the exchange only 2 per cent below par. Such a recovery after January, 1926 was, however, not accomplished by the lowering of prices alone but, perhaps more, by an element of speculation. The government's frequent shipments of gold to the United States were taken by exchange speculators as the sign of Japan's intention of returning to the gold standard. The recovery was, therefore, very rapid, until April, 1927 when, due to bank failure, the exchange again dropped 5 per cent in less than two months.

In the case of the Chinese exchange in Japan, the slump of 1924 was also remarkable. Although the price of silver fluctuated within the range of 33.⅛ to 31.½ pence, our tael exchange on Shanghai was speculated down from 60 to 49.¼ taels per Y. 100. This was apparently due to the slump of yen exchange on New York and London. However, after September, 1925 the price of silver gradually declined. Coupled with the recovery of yen exchange on New York and London, the cheapness of silver made the tael exchange in Japan to rise quite rapidly. In September, 1925 the highest quotation on Shanghai was Tls. 51.¾. This was raised to Tls. 81.½ in March, 1927.

The same thing can be said of the Bombay exchange in Japan. In October, 1923, the average demand rate on Bombay was Rs. 157 per Y. 100. This was successively slumped down to Rs. 108.6 in February, 1925. But from March on, the yen began to improve, largely because of the decline in the price of silver and the rise in the yen exchange on New York and London.

3. GREAT EXCESS OF COMMODITY IMPORTS

The excess of imports was heaviest in 1924 as reconstruction materials were urgently needed. The total of such excess of commodity imports during three years was 1,212 million yen as follows:

JAPAN'S COMMODITY TRADE AFTER THE EARTHQUAKE[1]
(million yen)

	Exports	*Imports*	*Excess of imports*	*4% correction*	*Balance*
1924	1,871	2,597	-726	103	-623
1925	2,377	2,738	-357	109	-248
1926	2,118	2,561	-443	102	-341
			-1,526		-1,212

On the other hand, gold has been shipped to America in order to peg the exchange. Notice below the heavy exports of gold in 1926. On the whole, however, the trade was most gloomy in 1924 as the following trade statistics show.

SPECIE MOVEMENT AFTER THE EARTHQUAKE
(million yen)

	Exports	*Imports*	*Excess*
1924	—	4	-4
1925	22	-	22
1926	35	1	34
			52

JAPAN'S VISIBLE TRADE AFTER THE EARTHQUAKE

	Excess of Imports	*4% Correction*	*Excess of specie Exports*	*Final Visible Trade Balance*
1924	-726	103	-4	-627
1925	-357	109	22	-226
1926	-443	102	34	-307
				-1,160

[1] Department of Finance, *Kinyu Jikō*, 1925, pp. 221-238, and its subsequent quarterly reports. Figures include Chosen and Taiwan.

Thus, the commodity trade for 3 years after the great earthquake shows an excess of imports by 1,212 million yen against which a net of 52 million yen was paid back in gold, making a total deficit of 1,160 million yen.

In normal years, the excess of these visible imports was paid back by invisible receipts. But the invisible receipts for these three years were also decreased. The result was a heavy net loss to Japan amounting to 706 million yen as follows:

JAPAN'S INVISIBLE TRADE AFTER THE EARTHQUAKE[1]
(million yen)

Credit	*1924*	*1925*	*1926*[2]
1. Interests and dividends receivable	20	19	18
2. Profits and remittances receivable	123	148	140
3. Freights and the like receivable	185	196	170
4. Premiums by insurance companies	104	117	100
5. Tourists expenditures in Japan	48	47	47
6. Government's income abroad	24	21	15
7. Miscellaneous	15	17	14
Total	520	565	504
Debit			
1. Interests and dividends payable	82	106	100
2. Profits and services payable	7	7	7
3. Freights and the like payable	68	67	67
4. Premiums payable	89	97	85
5. Japanese tourists abroad	29	27	27
6. Interests and other payments by the government	81	87	98
7. Miscellaneous	1	4	
Total	357	295	384
Net Balance	164	170	120

[1] Based on the Finance Department's Quarterly Report of Financial and Economic Conditions in Japan, no. 4 and 5. The government began lately to report this kind of statistics running as far back as 1923.

[2] My conservative estimates. They roughly correspond to those which were made by the Tokio Chamber of Commerce, *The Kokumin Shimbun*, March 4, 1927.

JAPAN'S TRADE BALANCE AFTER THE EARTHQUAKE

	1924	1925	1926	Total
Visible Trade Balance	−627	−226	−307	−1,160
Invisible Trade Balance	164	170	120	454
Net Loss	−463	—56	−187	−706

The reasons for these unfavorable balances are obvious. In spite of unfavorable rates of exchange for imports, the needs of reconstruction materials were so pressing that imports soon swelled rapidly and far outbalanced exports. However, one must not hastily conclude that that was the only cause for the net exchange slump of 1925. There were other and more immediate and contributing causes. But it suffices here to note that the swelling of imports was chiefly due to the reconstruction needs necessitated by the earthquake devastation.

4. CAPITAL IMPORTS

The loss of 706 million yen was again paid back mainly by capital borrowing. Japan borrowed 566 million yen in 1924, 186 million yen in 1925 and 101 million yen in 1926, making a total floating of 853 million yen loans at London and New York [1] in three years. The sale of Japanese domestic bonds and stocks to foreign countries was also enormous.[2]

In February 1924 alone the government had floated a 6½ per cent dollar loan amounting to a total face value of 150 million dollars in New York and a 6 per cent sterling loan of 25 million pounds sterling in London in order to redeem in part, a 4½ per cent sterling loan of the first and

[1] The reports of the Tokio Chamber of Commerce, *The Kokumin Shimbun*, March 9, 1927.

[2] The interest rates were still high in Japan without much difference since November 1919 when the Bank of Japan last raised its discount rates up to 8.03%. Therefore, the domestic bonds were cheap and were exported considerably. The interest rates began to decline very slowly only after October, 1926.

second series, and in part, to purchase materials and supplies for the reconstruction. 7 per cent Daido Electric Company's bonds ($15 million) and 6 per cent Industrial Bank's bonds ($22 million) were also floated during this year. In 1925 bonds of electric Companies such as 6 per cent Tokio Electric ($24 million), 7 per cent Toho Electric ($15 million), 7 per cent Ujikawa Electric ($14 million), 6½ per cent Daido Electric ($13.5 million) and 6 per cent second Tokio Electric were floated, nearly all in New York. In 1926, 6 per cent Toho Electric ($10 million) and 5½ per cent Tokio City (£6 million) bonds, as well as 5½ per cent Tokio City ($20 million) and 6 per cent Yokohama City bonds of 1927 were also floated in New York and London. All these capital movements may be seen below.

CAPITAL MOVEMENT AFTER THE EARTHQUAKE[1]
(million yen)

Credit	*1924*	*1925*	*1926*[2]	*Total*
1. Investments of foreigners in Japan	566	186	101	
2. Realizing foreign investments by Japanese	104	60	80	
3. Miscellaneous	18	...	...	
Total	688	246	181	
4. Sales of domestic bonds, stocks and the decrease in bankers' funds abroad * ...	207	15	156	
Total credits	895	261	337	1,493
Debit				
1. Realizing of investments by foreigners..	336	104	100	
2. Japanese investments abroad	96	101	50	
Total debits	432	205	150	787
Excess of credits	463	56	187	706

[1] Based on the quarterly Reports of the Finance Department.

[2] As the government figures for 1926 have not yet come out, the figures for 1926 and the footnote * under Credits are my conservative estimates. *Vide supra*, p. 64. These are, however, partly based on the Reports of the Tokio Chamber of Commerce, as reported by *The Kokumin Shimbun*, March 8, 9, 10, 11, 1927.

Thus the deficit of 706 million yen was paid back by capital borrowing, sale of domestic bonds, etc., the complete account of which may be seen below.

BALANCE OF INTERNATIONAL PAYMENTS, 1924-1926
(million yen)

Credit	*1924*	*1925*	*1926*	*Total*
I. Exports of merchandise	...	...	...	
Exports of gold and silver	...	22	34	
II. Freight and other invisible receipts	164	170	120	
III. Foreign investments in Japan	566	186	101	
Realizing of Japanese investments abroad	104	60	80	
Sales of domestic bonds, etc.	207	15	156	
Miscellaneous	...	...	...	
Total credits	1,059	453	491	2,003
Debit				
I. Imports of merchandise (net excess)	623	248	341	
Imports of gold and silver	4	...	...	
II. Invisible net payments	...	...	...	
III. Realizing of investments by foreigners	336	104	100	
Japanese investments abroad	96	101	50	
Total debits	1,059	453	491	2,003

These were commercial transactions. Apart from these, there has been a great deal of speculative buying and selling of exchange, the amount of which must have been considerable as there were many elements of speculation during this period.

5. PEGGING AND SALE OF GOLD FUNDS

When Finance Minister J. Inoue saw exchange fall off by 3 per cent in November and 7 per cent in December, he at once changed his former policy and began to peg exchanges by selling gold funds abroad and let the Yokohama Specie Bank maintain the rate of 1 per cent below par in November and an average of 2½ per cent below par in December 1923.

Therefore, the gaps created between the rates of foreigners' exchange banks and the Yokohama Specie Bank were already $1.00 in November and $3.00 in December. In January, 1924 when the Yamamoto cabinet changed to the Kinyoura cabinet, Finance Minister Shoda began a more vigorous selling of foreign funds at a desired pegged rate of exchange. In February he floated a 6½ per cent dollar loan and a 6 per cent sterling loan amounting to a total face value of 550 million yen, but the real net receipt was only 470 millien yen, yielding over 7 per cent interest. Even at the expense of such " nationally disgraceful " loans he then publicly announced a free policy of selling foreign funds. But his free policy was no more free than Takahashi's or Ickiki's; it was only more free than Inoue's. He still insisted on the restriction imposed on exchange banks by limiting the amount of letters of credit, thus restricting the volume of imports. He also suspended the report of gold holdings abroad, presumably thinking that speculation could thereby be minimized. But the result was contrary to his expectation. Speculation was still wild, and the exchange was moving from bad to worse. Meanwhile, the Kiyoura cabinet ran on a rock; and a general election took place. Exchange was one of the burning issues of the day which were put at the general election. The Jitsugyo Doshi-kai or the Businessmen's Party headed by Mr. Y. Muto was advocating the immediate and complete lifting of the gold embargo while the three opposition parties were advocating a more lenient policy of selling gold funds. But none of them had the right attitude. For to advocate the former, one had to become aware of a sudden fall of 20 per cent of all imported goods and also those goods which were dependent on imported materials. In order to avoid this sudden fall some, like Dr. M. Takayanagi of the Osaka Chamber of Commerce, advocated a certain length of preparatory period before the final action should take place. But this sort of argument without taking heed of the relative price situation took it for granted that the exchange moved in a simple mechanical fashion, believing that the lifting of the gold embargo was the sole remedy for all diseases. But to advocate the latter policy, one had to meet a still graver question, for in order to sell the gold funds at a desired pegged rate there must be first enough funds available abroad. Yet to raise any more funds by floating foreign loans at such a high yield as 7 per cent as in the case of the flotation in February, 1924 would certainly not be approved by the people. It was at this time that the writer first made public his " step theory of raising foreign exchanges ", which will be discussed later in this chapter. However, in this political race the Kensei-Kai Party with its professed policy of retrenchment and readjustment won the election, and the Kato cabinet with Finance Minister Hamaguchi came into existence in June, 1924. Nevertheless, the exchange became still worse. In October it reached the lowest point of $38.50 in Japan, and remained there until February, 1925 when it began to recover.

Now Hamaguchi's exchange policy was at first not known. But in December, 1924 at the Annual Kansai Bankers Meeting and on January 23, 1925 at the Diet he openly made it known that he was going to export gold whenever that seemed feasible. Thus at last the Finance Minister put his finger on the hitherto neglected or rather scrupulously guarded spot, and began to report the gold holdings abroad after one year's suspension. Meanwhile his policy of fiscal as well as of financial retrenchment [1] began to show its effects.

[1] His announced policy was that the correctives of exchanges should be preceded by the fiscal adjustment and retrenchment of the government which is the largest consumer in Japan and sets an example to the public. Accordingly the budget for 1925 was cut with radical readjustments, and over 68 million yen were saved, besides the postponement of undertakings amounting to 84 million yen in General Expenditures, mak-

Prices were first declining, exports were encouraged and exchange was steadily recovering. In matters of export trade, he encouraged the formation of manufacturers' unions of export goods and of exporters' unions to which the government was authorized to advance capital with a low rate of interest. More effective than these trade encouragements were, of course, exports of gold. The government actually exported in a number of shipments 22 million yen during 1925 and 35 million yen during 1926. These specie shipments were conspicuous. And they appeared more so to the eyes of exchange speculators. Thus speculation again took place and helped to restore the exchange rather more swiftly than was expected.

6. CAUSES OF EXCHANGE SLUMPS OF 1924

So far we have seen that the causes of the exchange slump of 1924 were (1) exchange speculation, (2) sudden excessive imports, (3) draining of gold funds abroad, (4) cumulative failures of industrial firms and banks since the depression of 1920, intensified by a great financial loss of the earthquake and (5) failure of government's exchange policy. Of these, (1) exchange speculation and (2) the sudden excessive imports were the two must influential and striking causes. The chief sources of exchange speculation were (a) draining of gold funds abroad, (b) unbalanced payments chiefly due to excessive imports, (c) earthquake loss, (d) lack of a definite exchange policy on the part of the government. The reasons for the sudden excessive imports were due to (a) reconstruction needs necessitated by the earthquake and not

ing the total of 152 million yen cut from the budget. Likewise, in Special Account more than 104 million yen were adjusted and reduced from the budget. In the formation of the budget for 1926, the same spirit of economy was followed, while the policy of restricting the issue of domestic loans within 150 million yen was strictly observed in both years of 1925 and 1926.

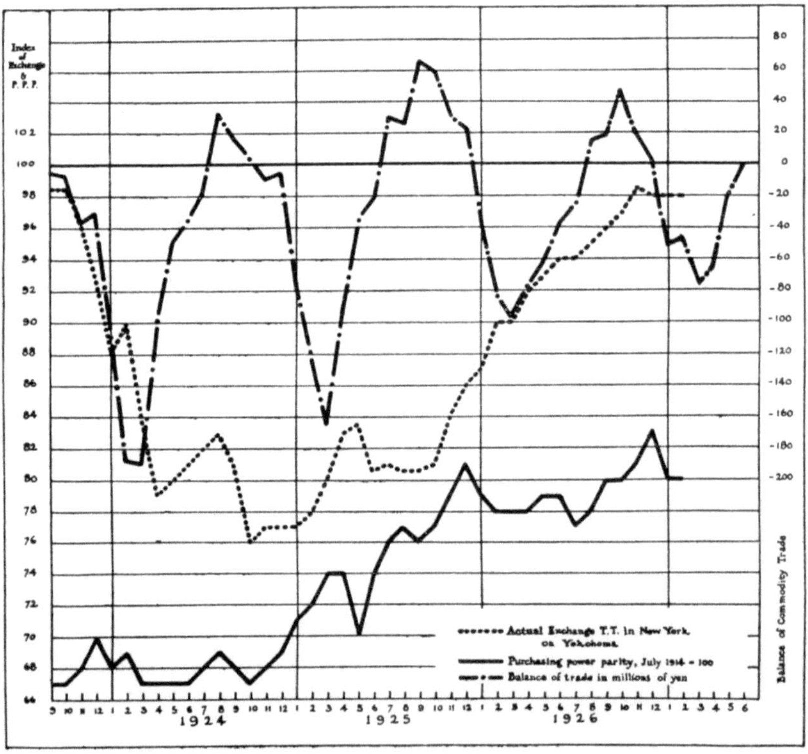

CHART XI. PURCHASING POWER PARITY, EXCHANGES AND BALANCE OF TRADE AFTER THE GREAT EARTHQUAKE

(b) relatively high prices in Japan during 1924, as some writers are inclined to argue. For instance, G. C. Allen, British consul at Nagoya, having seen the note expansion in Japan after the earthquake, an obvious fact, and the high level of prices in Japan, hastily concluded that high prices were the direct cause of exchange slumps of 1924,[1] admitting, however, that there was no very "*close* correspondence" between exchanges and the purchasing power parities "as prices were taken from wholesale prices." But such an allegation ignores wholly the facts of price movement. It was true that prices were moving slightly higher after the earthquake. But after January, 1924 when exchanges were dropping fearfully, prices were also dropping, although in July, 1924 they were again a bit higher. But on the whole, after the earthquake and during 1924, prices were neither very much lower nor higher.[2] Furthermore, what is more important is the relative price movement. The curve showing the purchasing power parity of the yen in terms of the dollar after the earthquake and during 1924, shown in the accompanying Chart XI clearly proves the point that a high level of prices in Japan was not in conformity with the dropping of the exchange curve.[3]

Among the factors causing exchange speculation, the draining of gold funds abroad was most influential and striking. Except in March, 1924 when the government reported the gold holding abroad as only 292 million yen, similar reports were completely suspended during the year. This action by the government clearly shows that the government was also of the opinion that the draining of gold funds

[1] G. C. Allen, "Recent Currency and Exchange Policy of Japan," *Economic Journal*, March, 1925, pp. 81-83.

[2] *See* Chart X, p. 139.

[3] Sources of Chart XI are same as Chart III and VIII. They were all previously given.

abroad was one of the chief sources of exchange speculation, and therefore refrained from reporting them.

Another way to prove the importance of this element in the exchange speculation is to suppose that the earthquake came in September 1, 1919 instead of September 1, 1923, and see what might have happened under the circumstances when gold funds abroad were most abundant. As was already explained, during the period of the Great War, Japan gained 1,292 million yen in trade and 1,333 million yen in invisible trade, making a total profit of 2,625 million yen, 1,135 million yen of which were held abroad as gold funds jointly by the government and the Bank of Japan at the end of 1918. Moreover, exchange bankers had more than 500 million yen of their own exchange funds abroad. Therefore, even if the calamity which befell in September 1, 1919 caused similar excess of imports like that of 1924 by 726 million yen, the excess could be easily met by the gold funds, as there were at this time (August 31, 1923) 1,354 million yen in funds. It would be highly improbable that there would be any broad speculation that would cause as great a slump as 24 per cent in exchange; 2 or 3 per cent would be the maximum drop. But unfortunately the disaster came in 1923. And the meagre gold funds then existing were taken as if they were the immediate objective or th ebarometer to which exchange speculators and the Japanese government alike turned their attention. It was only after February, 1925 that the government actually began to export domestic gold to stabilize and to eventually restore the exchange.

7. REASONS FOR RECOVERY

The exchange recovery of 1925 was, however, largely due to relatively lower prices in Japan. Chart XI (page 149) shows that first the purchasing power parity began to move upward. This was followed by a gradual improvement in trade and actual exchange, showing a pretty close correlation. But the exchange recovery of 1926 was more rapid and steeper than that of purchasing power parity,[1] showing again that there was a *confidence* on the part of exchange dealers in the Japanese yen [2] and an *expectation* of the final restoration of the gold standard as in the case of Great Britain in 1925.

The fall in the general level of prices in Japan after January, 1925 may be chiefly accounted for by the retrenchment policy of the Kensei-kai government. This policy not only discouraged the note expansion by exporting gold but also contracted various forms of credits already mentioned.

The falling of prices, however, was not welcomed by certain bankers who abnormally extended their credits when prices were moving upward. And the cases of bank failure temporarily increased, and a few percent drop of exchange were expected. But from the standpoint of national credit and national exportability based on the real strength of industry, the fall of prices at least to the levels of Great Britain and U. S. A. was highly desirable. It meant more exports, more invisible receipts and the final return to the gold standard which would make it possible to abandon the much-abused practice of artificial pegging.

8. BANK FAILURE OF APRIL 1927

Outwardly the economic situation in Japan in the first half of 1927 was getting better. While prices remained almost stationary, the usual excess of commodity imports for the first half year was only 268 million yen as compared to 403 and 517 million yen for 1926 and 1925 respectively. But

[1] *Vide supra*, Chart XI, p. 149.

[2] It is estimated that the Shanghai speculators alone bought the future delivery of yen to the amount of over 200 million yen in expectation of her return to the gold standard. J. Inoue, *Japan's Economic and Financial Situations after the War*, Tokio, 1925, p. 168.

underneath there was a tendency of uneasiness and worry, especially among Tokio bankers who happened to have many million yens of bills still unsettled because of the earthquake. The total amount of such bills at this time was 270 million yen. And one-half of this amount, according to the present Finance Minister, Mr. Mitsuchi, was in the hand of the Bank of Taiwan. In order to readjust these bills, the government again introduced in the Diet the necessary measure, which later was much obstructed by the opposition party, the Seiyakai. The attacks and interpellations of the opposition party went beyond what was necessary. They demanded that the government disclose names of the banks holding these earthquake bills and names of the bankers who were connected in drafting such measure. Finance Minister, Mr. Kataoka, answered such questions to some extent. Newspapers were wildly reporting these interpellations and answers at the Diet. The public soon became uneasy and began to suspect the inner conditions of the second and third class banks. Hasty persons began a run on the banks. This was reported sensationally by the newspapers. Thus the Tokio Watanabe Bank and its affiliated bank, the Akaji Savings Bank, which were known to be most shaky, closed their doors on the 15th of March. This led to runs on many other banks, such as the Nakai Bank, Eighty-fourth Bank, Nakazawa Bank, Soda Bank, and Murai Bank. The total deposit in these 7 banks alone was over 200 million yen.[1] The depositors were mostly workers and people of the lower class.

Having failed in the Diet, the government was then trying to rescue the Bank of Taiwan which was then in trouble by issuing an urgency Imperial ordinance. But unfortunately, this was rejected by the Privy Council. This action by the Privy Council at the critical moment made the financial situa-

[1] The Asahi English Supplement, *Present Day Japan*, 1927, p. 88.

tion still worse. Now the big banks such as the Bank of Taiwan and the Fifteenth Bank had to close their doors. The failure of the Bank of Taiwan was partly due to the failure of Suzuki & Co. and the Kawasaki Dockyard, which were indiscriminately expanding business and failed to readjust themselves after the War and, especially, after the great earthquake. It is said that Suzuki & Co. alone owed the Bank of Taiwan 350 out of 450 million yen loans (including earthquake bills) at the time of difficulty. The Sixty-fourth Bank of Kobe, the Omi Bank of Osaka and many other small banks closed their doors during this stage in April. The total number of bank failures was 29. The deposits in these banks were estimated to have been 800 million yen.[1] The Wakatsuki cabinet, taking the responsibility, finally resigned; and on the 20th of April the Seiyukai cabinet headed by Mr. Tanaka was formed. A three week's moratorium was then ordered. Meanwhile, a special session of the Diet was convened; two bills were passed, one relating to the indemnity the government was to give the Bank of Japan to the extent of 500 million yen in case the Bank incurred the loss by giving special accomodation to those banks that might fall into trouble after the termination of the moratorium. The big banks of Tokio also came to an understanding that in case of need they would accommodate bills to end the panic. And thus ended the panic, the moratorium, and the run, without any of the things feared happening. This was the middle of May, 1927.

This financial panic, however, reflected itself immediately in exchange rates. During April the yen lost one dollar on New York, a half penny on London, and in May one dollar fifty cents on New York and 11/16 penny on London. But since the end of May it is again recovering. The total ex-

[1] J. Inoue, "Present Financial Condition," *Jitsugyono Nippon*, Tokio, July, 1927, p. 240.

change slump during these two months was 5 per cent. This was clearly due to exchange speculation, for prices remained the same, the trade was even getting better and there was no big capital movement during these months.

9. SUMMARY

Thus the period 1924-1927, from the point of view of the general economic situation, is a continuation of the post-war period. Prices were comparatively high in Japan. The excess of imports was still great. Realizing of foreign investments, draining of gold funds, and fresh borrowing were logical consequences. This bad situation was intensified by the great earthquake. Exchange speculation was, therefore, the natural outcome. The slump of 1924 and the rapid recovery in 1926 were remarkable in that they presented a case where exchanges were first and mostly influenced by speculation rather than by relative prices or the balance of payments. That is to say, the slump and recovery were relatively more rapid than the corresponding movement of prices or the balance of payments.

The bank and business failures of March and April, 1927 have clearly shown that Japan's financial organization and her banking system were not quite adequate. More co-ordination of banking funds under some central bank and a desire that the Bank of Japan should assume more responsibility at such crises were keenly felt.

From the point of view of exchange policy, the government's failure reached a climax in 1924. It was only after 1925 that the government gradually began to reduce the gold reserve at home by specie exports. This had two effects: it served to peg the exchange, and it slowly and gradually lowered the general level of prices, which eventually served also to restore the exchange.

But in financing foreign trade, nothing has yet been done

or introduced. Acceptances and a discount market are still non-existent. Even the "stamped bill" once introduced is now not used. There is as yet no co-ordination between exchange banks and home banks. In fact, there is yet, strictly speaking, no specialized exchange bank. The so-called exchange banks are engaging in all kinds of business—from deposits to trust business. The consequence is that their financing power of foreign trade is very much limited and is not smooth and fluid as it should be. Of course, there is no foreign investment banking.

In general, foreign banking in Japan is still in its infancy, and it is rather backward when compared with the growth of her trade and international payments. The necessity of banking reform, then, belongs to the immediate future.

CHAPTER VI

Conclusion: Characteristics of Yen Exchange Fluctuations and Their Correctives

I. CHARACTERISTICS OF YEN EXCHANGE FLUCTUATIONS

We have seen in the foregoing analysis of yen exchange movements that there have been two noteworthy characteristics in yen exchange fluctuations. The first has to do with the nature of Japan's foreign trade, the second is concerned with her "pegging" policy. In the first characteristic there are (1) seasonal fluctuations as well as (2) general trade prosperity fluctuations. Thus we have seen that as a rule, Japan's trade is unfavorable in the first half of the year when she imports cotton heavily, and favorable in the latter half of the year when she exports raw silk heavily. This seasonal trade movement, as in the case of British-American trade [1] tends to influence the exchange rates, especially the dollar exchange. Exchange fluctuations resulting from this factor, however, are generally considered to be within a range of a few points. The seasonal movement, therefore, offers no great problem. But the most important factor has been

[1] As a consequence of heavy exports of cotton and wheat, "the exchange is normally in favor of America during the last five months of the year and against it in the first seven". Hartley Withers, *Money Changing, London*, 1913, p. 76.

the general trade prosperity of the country.[1] Japan is not yet a great maritime country as Great Britain is,[2] nor a

[1] The general trade prosperity can be judged by the following statistics.

THE FIRST PERIOD

	1914	1915	1916	1917	1918	Total
Net balance of visible trade......	22	211	245	380	334	1,292
Net balance of invisible trade....	— 6	69	277	415	578	1,333
Net earning	16	280	622	795	912	2,625

THE SECOND PERIOD

	1919	1920	1921	1922	1923	Total
Net balance of visible trade......	—408	—787	—502	—256	—533	—2,486
Net balance of invisible trade....	504	420	195	154	169	1,445
Net deficit	96	—367	—307	—102	—364	—1,041

THE THIRD PERIOD

	1924	1925	1926	Total	Grand Total
Net balance of visible trade......	—627	—226	—307	—1,160	—2,554
Net balance of invisible trade....	164	170	120	454	3,252
Not deficit.............	—463	— 56	—187	— 706	878

[2] Japan in 1923 had 3,046 steamships, totalling 3,321,071 gross tons. The government's subsidy that year for the three largest steamship companies alone was over 6 million yen. Yet N. Y. K., the largest steamship company, earned only Y 2,732,000 against its paid-up capital of 58 million yen and 17 million yen reserve. O. S. K. earned Y 1,205,000 against its paid-up capital of 62.5 million yen and 17 million yen reserve, while T. K. K. lost Y 5,443,000 against its paid-up capital of 22.7 million

great investing country as France was before the War, or as the United States is after the War.[1] Japan's international balance of payments is largely controlled by her trade prosperity which in turn is largely controlled by the amount of the exports of silk and cotton goods[2] which in turn are largely determined by prices. This was especially the case for the first three periods, namely, (1) immediately before 1914, (2) during the War, and (3) after the War to 1923, although the causes for high or low prices differed according to each of these periods. Before the War, overflotation of both domestic and foreign loans was the chief cause of relatively high prices at home and an unfavorable balance of payments. Consequently, the yen exchange tended to decline. During the War, relatively high prices abroad or relatively low prices at home were the dominant cause of a better balance of payments. Therefore we had high rates of exchange. Conversely, when Japanese prices became relatively much higher after the War, the exchange again tended to decline. Thus the trade prosperity factor has been inherently working in Japanese exchange.

yen, and 2.5 million yen reserve. (Department of Finance, *Kinyu Jikō*, 1924, pp. 210-212). In 1922 the British Empire had 20,106 steamships, representing 12,913,000 tons. The United Kingdom alone had 12,787 steamships with 11,223,000 tons. (*The Statesman's Year Book for 1925*, London, 1925, p. 93.)

[1] Before the War, France was the second leading creditor nation, only surpassed by Great Britain. The annual flotation of foreign loans in France before 1914, was from three to five billion gold francs. This meant that she was able to lend foreign countries more than 80% of her total loans floated. (*See* figures in George W. Edwards, *Investing in Foreign Securities*, New York, 1926, p. 95.)

U. S. A. had floated about 10 billion dollars for the Allied countries during the War, and about 19 billion dollars more after the War, during the five years of 1919 to 1923. (*See ibid.*, pp. 58-60.)

[2] The amounts of raw silk, cotton tissue, and other silk and cotton goods usually occupy 63 to 66% of whole exports.

But after the great earthquake speculation was largely responsible for the undue slump of the exchange, for we have already seen that during this period the price movement was *relatively* constant. Such slumps as 20 to 24 per cent below par and a great divergence from the purchasing power parity were primarily caused by the alarms of the exchange dealers over the gloomy aspects of Japan's trade after the earthquake, and more especially over the drained exchange funds kept abroad.

With this we have already come to discuss our second characteristic of yen exchange fluctuations. For the "pegging" of exchange by means of gold funds has been peculiar in the Japanese exchange,[1] and has caused less stabilization and many speculative fluctuations. Thus before, during and after the War the yen was abnormally pegged down,[2] while after the earthquake the yen was abnormally speculated down because of the inadequacy of her pegging system. Furthermore, the pegging has been the cause of the making of mistakes by the various inexperienced or wrongly biased Finance Ministers, while it has given a substantial ground for foreigners to speculate in exchange.

[1] It is singular in the Japanese exchange, because Japan is not a gold exchange standard country as are the Philippine Islands or India. Peggings by Great Britain, France, Belgium and other European states are merely temporary, whereas Japan's pegging by means of exchange funds has been customary.

[2] The case here is just the opposite of European pegged exchanges. In Europe, notably in Great Britain, France and Italy, actual exchanges were much higher than purchasing power parities because of the "managed" exchanges during the war. But after the War, like the Japanese exchange, European exchanges were much speculated down. *Cf.* Chart III, VIII, XI with U. S. Senate Commission on Gold and Silver Inquiry, *ibid.*, Chart XIII, XXII, XXX, etc.

2. DEFECTS IN EXCHANGE BANKING

We have also seen from the foregoing analysis that the exchange banking in Japan is still in its infant stage. Strictly speaking, the Bank of Japan is not the bank of banks, nor the bank of exchange banks. Before the War it loaned 40 to 50 per cent, during the War 60 to 80 per cent, after the War again 40 to 50 per cent of its total loans, on foreign exchange bills alone. But it is generally considered that 80 per cent of these loans were simply made for one institution, namely, the Yokohama Specie Bank, under a special arangement. Other exchange bankers did not always find it profitable to borrow funds from the central bank on exchange bills, as the Bank's rate was lower for bonds than for commercial bills.[1] Moreover, the Bank has entirely failed in directing the surplus of domestic funds to the needs of financing foreign trade and in directing the surplus of foreign funds to the needs of financing domestic trade and industries. And thus having less contact with the money market, the bank's official rate has never led the market rate. On the contrary, it always followed the market rate, thus losing its important position in the market.[2] These defects of central banking were frequently aggravated by the dominance of the Finance Minister over the governor of the Bank of Japan. For instance, in fixing the rates of interest on loans, on excess issues, or in extending credits, or in the use of Bank's exchange funds abroad, Finance Ministers

[1] Nominally the discount rate for commercial paper and the rate for loans on bonds were the same. But in reality they favored loans on bonds. Only last March 1927, they made discount rates on commercial papers lower than those on bonds.

[2] Besides inability to control other banks financially, the Bank of Japan has no right to supervise or to collect reports from other banks. The Department of Finance has the supervisory power over banks, but most of these regulatory powers, which are only formal limitations, were made in 1890 or 37 years ago.

were too powerful and acted more according to their own partisan interests than according to the sound principles of banking.

Exchange bankers were also handicapped by the absence of extensive use of bank acceptances and an adequate discount market.[1] Therefore, there was no means of coordination among such banks, and more particularly among the exchange banks and the commercial banks.

In financing imports, the use of yen bills has been fostered. But the amount of such bills is yet insufficient to establish any specialized discount house on a commercial basis. Foreign interest-bearing bills are still found in great bulk.

The Yokohama Specie Bank, for instance, had in its portfolio such interest bills amounting to from 20 to 40 per cent of the total advances it has made in recent years.[2] And these are mostly kept in the exchange bank's portfolio until maturity, as there is no adequate means of disposing of them.

[1] The reasons why acceptances are not much used and the discount market is not yet developed may be summarized as follows: (1) Our business men are still sticking to the old way of doing business secretly. They do not like to inform or to let it be known to bankers exactly what their credit standings are or what transactions they are handling, etc., etc. (2) There is yet no reliable organization or system for credit investigation. True we have "koshinjos" or credit investigating firms. But they are no more dependable than quack newspapers or trade journals. (3) There are no acceptance houses such as are found in London. Therefore, trade bills do not circulate. (4) There is a fear of over-accepting finance bills through various methods of evasion even if some rigid regulations were enacted. (5) Lastly, our bankers are too self-sufficient. That is to say that they dislike the idea of rediscounting the bills which were once accepted, even if these bills were "stamped" by the Bank of Japan. The remedies for the above may be (a) more education for bankers and business men concerning the new instruments, (b) carefully prepared enactment concerning the use of such instruments.

[2] *See* Department of Finance, *Kinyu Jikō*, Tokio, 1924, p. 93.

In financing exports the Bank of Japan's " stamped bills " were once temporarily used in order to relieve the tightened foreign trade financing. But the bills, which had no public market, had to disappear soon, when another financial policy was adopted by the next Finance Minister.

In addition to the defects of the central banking and of the exchange market, individual exchange banks in Japan are not, strictly speaking, exchange banks at all, for they deal with all kinds of banking business. The result is, their funds are easily tied up with long-term investments in industires, agriculture and colonial exploitation, and are very easily frozen up. Such diversified interests have made the exchange banks extremely weak when they needed a concentration of funds in order to meet industrial failures.[1]

3. EFFECTS OF YEN EXCHANGE FLUCTUATIONS

From the foregoing survey we have witnessed how the balance of payments and speculation have acted on exchange, and how exchanges have reacted on trade and remittances. For instance, in trade the fall of yen exchange tended to encourage exports and discourage imports, and the rise of yen exchange tended to encourage imports and discourage exports, and the rise of silver encouraged exports and discouraged imports, as the fall or rise of exchanges did not go with the rise and fall of prices at the same time and in the same degree. Furthermore, the fall of exchange necessitated that the Japanese should pay more for remittances as the exchanges did not coincide with the value of currency, besides causing the fall of Japanese bonds abroad. To illustrate, the high yield of the Japanese loans of 1924 was largely responsible for the yen exchange slump at the time.

[1] It is well here to mention that a banking reform, both central and local, is now being seriously contemplated by the government. The committees for the Monetary Reform (Kinyu-chosa-kai) were already appointed by the fall of 1926, and are now making investigations.

As there was no free movement of gold after 1917, nor a sufficient selling of gold funds after 1919, exchange fluctuations became greater and greater, causing a disturbance in the price situation. Some industries, whose raw materials were dependent on imported goods, such as cotton mills, were most hard hit. Many went into bankruptcy, while the remaining ones cut their outputs one-half.

Exports, however, were encouraged. Physically, for instance, much raw silk was exported. But, pecuniarily, Japan lost a great deal, for her prices remained relatively constant while the exchanges were driven down abnormally by speculation. In other words, we had to export relatively more for a smaller amount of foreign goods and services simply because of truly unfavorable rates of exchange. Furthermore, if it were not for the fact that the exchange reacted on prices and thereby caused numerous industrial bankruptcies and bank failures, the Japanese would not have raised such a "cry of national peril and danger" during 1924-1925. It was precisely for this fact that the exchange correctives were honestly sought in Japan.

4. REFORM OF EXCHANGE BANKING

In the first place, the Bank of Japan should be reformed in such a way that it can truly remain as the central coordinator of banking funds. It should take a more active part in controlling credits by lowering or raising discount rates and by buying and selling exchange bills.[1] Moreover, the Bank of Japan should not be subordinated to the opinion of the Finance Minister; but there should be financial cooperation such as that maintained between the Treasury Department and the Federal Reserve Board in America.[2]

[1] At present the Bank does not operate in the open market other than by its loans and discounts.

[2] H. Parker Willis and William H. Steiner, *Federal Reserve Banking Practice*, New York, 1926, pp. 9-10.

The use of bank acceptances and the development of discount markets should at the same time be fostered. And in order to do so, the practice in business transactions should be improved so that more commercial paper can be used by merchants with the idea of discounting them at the banks, and encouraging the establishment of regular discount houses as the true discounters of the commercial paper, not only among exchange and other bankers, but also between merchants and bankers.

The practice of sound banking should also be observed by the individual exchange bankers. Too much credit should not be extended either in time or in the field where exchange bankers had better terminate their business in favor of industrial or other commercial bankers so that their funds may properly remain within the sphere of exchange banking. Also, too much credit should not be granted to any one firm.

With such a view of reform in mind, the present Bank Laws and the Bill Laws should be completely revised and systematized.

5. CORRECTIVES FOR YEN EXCHANGE FLUCTUATIONS

We have seen that the balance of payments and speculation have been the two most important factors causing fluctuations in the yen exchange.

A. Among the elements in the balance of payments, trade has been the predominant factor. And in trade, the relative price movement or the purchasing power parity of the yen, in turn, has been the determining factor in the long run. In order, therefore, to bring about a stabilization of the yen exchange, price stabilization should precede. Excessive state and local loans for non-economic purposes, whether to be floated at home or abroad, should very carefully be limited, as these soon tend to swell the country's credits and thereby to enhance prices. In other words, the recent rapid expansion of government expenditures in Japan should be greatly repressed. Even the economic undertakings, such as building of railroads, wharfs, roads, electric power plants, etc., should not be undertaken all at once. A proper distribution of floating debts both in time and amount is important in stabilizing general prices.

A careful limitation of note issue is also necessary. The present amount of security issue, guaranteed by the government, was raised to 120 million yen twenty-eight years ago (in 1899), and since then no change has been made, although the volume of trade has increased, generally speaking, more than eight times.[1] The result is that there has always been an excess issue amounting generally to over 100 million yen. Therefore, the limit of guaranteed security issue should be at least lifted to 220 million yen, and the excessive issue tax should be at least 1 per cent higher than the Bank's discount rate.[2]

The extension of credit by the central bank should also be made more favorable on the basis of commercial paper rather than on government bonds, so that inflation may be avoided in every possible way.

The adoption of an effective discount policy by the Bank of Japan is perhaps more fundamentally necessary than scores of petty reforms to control bank credit. As Mr. J. Inoue pointed out, it is true that the bank of Japan has nominally kept a discount policy by first lowering or raising interest rates according as the excess of exports or imports increased.[3] That is to say, if the excess of imports

[1] For instance, foreign trade in value was increased 9 times, production of raw silk 8 times, of cotton yarn 7 times, volume of note issue 10 times and check clearance over 100 times during these 28 years.

[2] The present excessive issue tax is 6%. But as the Bank's discount rate is often as high as 7.3%, the Bank prefers to pay tax and does not contract notes as flexibly as it should.

[3] J. Inoue, *Japan's Economic and Financial Situations, after the War*, Tokio, 1925, pp. 165-184.

continued for some time, the Bank raised its discount rate so that gold might not flow out, or if demand for capital was persistent and the market rate of interest was high, the Bank raised its discount rate so that any further expansion of bank credits might become impossible. This practice was more or less followed in the nineties when the volume of bank credit was comparatively small and the Bank was more competent in handling Japan's finance. But today the country's finance has outgrown the Bank of Japan. The Bank's loans other than those to the Yokohama Specie Bank are very small in ordinary time. The result is that the Bank's discount policy has become less effective. This was more so after the establishment of the gold embargo. Thus we saw that, although excess of imports was never more enormous than in the post-war period, the Bank had never raised its discount rate during the period of November, 1919 to April, 1925. The discount rate was fixed at 8.03 per cent. Gold was flowing in, but was not permitted to flow out. The expansion of credit was, therefore, unrestricted. Prices went up. Trade became unfavorable. Exchange was greatly dislocated.

On the other hand, if the Bank of Japan had adopted a more effective discount policy whereby bank credit was adequately controlled, giving out less sources for industrial failures and exchange speculation, the Japanese financial situation might have been less aggravated, and the great exchange slumps might have been avoided.

As pointed out before, prices do act intimately on foreign trade in Japan, because her chief exports consist of silk and cotton goods, the production of which is largely dependent upon the general level of prices. So in Japan in order to stabilize prices, the financial and currency reforms named seem indispensable.

We have seen that in Japan the general prosperity is much

dependent on her silk and cotton industries. As to the silk industry, the government has since 1926 encouraged the establishment of dry-cocoon warehouses by granting subsidies in order to stabilize the price of cocoons and to thus better finance the sericultural industry. Another measure which became effective after July 1, 1927 is the enforcement of raw silk transactions based on the "conditioned" weight. The "conditioned" weight means raw silk which contains 11 per cent of moisture, as that amount of moisture is absolutely necessary to keep the good qualities of raw silk. But heretofore, because of the climatic conditions of the country, the amount of moisture in raw silk was not uniform. The result was much dispute and ill-feeling between the domestic and foreign merchants. The measure was therefore timely, and will undoubtedly improve future transactions. The art of reeling has also made great advances in late years. The production of raw silk in Japan is also growing, the total amount for exports in 1926 being 57 million pounds, or almost 70 per cent of the total of the world's exports.[1] However, financing of the silk industry is not sufficiently improved. Herein lies another need for financial reform.

Regarding the price of raw silk, one will naturally think of artificial silk as the strong rival of raw silk. It is true that, while raw silk is more of an agricultural product and, being such, its price tends to increase, artificial silk is truly a manufactured article, and being such, its price tends to decrease. It is also true that to some extent artificial silk is displacing raw silk from older uses, as the price of the former is only about one-third of the price of the latter. This is why the rayon industry is rapidly growing. The total production of artificial silk of the world in 1926 is said to have far exceeded double the amount of raw silk. The

[1] The Silk Association of America, *The 27th Mid-year Report*, Sept., 1926, pp. 14-17.

United States alone produced that year more than 62 million pounds, while Japan produced 10 million pounds. But to a far greater extent, raw silk and artificial silk are complementary goods as the mixing of these two threads becomes more common. As a result of such use, it is found that the greater the demand for artificial silk the more raw silk was demanded. While, therefore, too much hope cannot be entertained in the future development of Japan's exports of raw silk, yet a proper encouragement of the raw silk industry is very important to increase her balance of trade.

During 1926 raw silk alone made up 36 per cent of total exports, while cotton yarn and cotton goods made up 26 per cent. On the other hand, 35 per cent of the year's imports were raw cotton, 45 per cent of which came from India and 40 per cent from the United States. The opinion that Japan's prosperity should be based upon the cotton industry is not without ground. It has better prospects than any other industry in Japan. Raw materials could easily be imported; its finished products are peculiarly suited to Oriental markets; and motive power and labor are plentiful. Under such circumstances the cotton industry has been firmly established. Its size in 1926 as given by the Cotton Spinners' Association of Japan was as follows:

	In 1926	In 1925
In Japan:		
Number of companies	53	53
Number of factories	234	233
Paid-up capital	$360,000,000	$351,000,000
Number of spindles	5,410,000	5,320,000
Dividend	14.8%	15.3%

	Spindles in 1926	Spindles over 1925
In China: (Those undertaken by the Japanese)		
Shanghai	950,072	3,152
Woosung	215,600	.....
Tsingtao	243,648	5,104
Hankow	24,816	2,456
South Manchuria	74,176	1,152
Total	1,318,312	11,864

Great obstacles to the cotton industry, however, are (1) the boycott against the Japanese goods by the Chinese, (2) disorder and tariff controversies in China, and (3) the unstable price of silver. These factors are not remediable by the Japanese alone; but how Japan acts toward China and other Oriental countries makes a great difference to trade and industries, especially the cotton industry in Japan.

Regarding the other exportable goods, such trade promoting organizations as Exporters' and Manufacturers' Associations[1] should be fostered more by the government so that her infant industries and trade may be better directed. But more fundamental in the long run is the increase of efficiency of labor, which alone enables the Japanese-made goods to compete with Western-made goods.

The balance of payments will also be re-enforced by the merger and the better management of shipping interests. The unnecessary competition among shipping companies in the past was detrimental to the expansion of Japan's maritime interests. In the future the overseas transportation merger or cartel with a proper governmental supervision

[1] Under a new law of 1925 for promoting exports, there have been already organized 5 Exporters' Associations and 33 Manufacturers' Associations.

seems to be the only solution against destructive foreign competition.

While Japanese immigrants' remittance cannot be expected to increase, Japanese *economic* interests in the Orient, especially in China, should be properly protected and promoted, as the income from these sources materially increases the credit side of the nation's balance sheet.[1]

B. Another important factor which has influenced the Japanese yen exchange is the element of speculation. We have observed that the pegging of exchange by the inexperienced government officials with relatively meager gold funds abroad was the constant cause of exchange speculation. When a Finance Minister showed his intention of buying exchange funds when the yen was high, the exchange was lowered by speculation. And when he began to sell these

[1] The Japanese investments in China, South Seas and Russia at the end of 1924 according to J. Inoue were as follows (million yen):

	Amount	Total	Grand Total
China:			
South Manchurian Railway and other private enterprises:			
1. In Manchuria	631.2		
2. Others	161.9	793.1	
Loans:			
1. Chinese Central Government	434.0		
2. Chinese Local Governments	18.0		
3. Private Loans	140.5	592.6	
South Seas:			
British Malay, British and Dutch India	108.8		
Investments in Philippine Islands	3.6		
Investments in South Seas Islands	21.3	133.9	
Russia:			
For munitions sold at the time of the War and still outstanding	70.2		
Russian Treasury Notes floated and still outstanding	221.6	291.9	1,811.7

funds at the time when the yen was below par, the exchange was abnormally pegged up.

Even during the same Finance Minister's policy of selling these funds, there had at one time been a more liberal selling, and at another time more restricted selling, all depending upon the fiscal conveniences of the time. Of course, such pegging has raised exchange rates many times. But the truth was that pegging was not the only means available. On the contrary, we have seen that Japan would have been much better situated if she had abolished such an exchange fund system entirely and let gold move, free from all artificial restrictions. For under free movements of gold, the Japanese currency would not have been so much inflated, and deflation would have taken place more promptly and without a great disturbance to business. And so with price stabilization, exchanges would also have been better stabilized. But instead of abolishing the exchange fund system, Japan kept at it, and went on pegging, and finally ushered in a great inflation, excess of importation, drainage of exchange funds, and specuation. The only correctives, therefore, against such speculations, are to abolish the exchange fund system entirely and return to the free movement of gold. The abolishment of the exchange fund system is simple and opportune at present, for there are no great funds left abroad now, and consequently there will be no problem of transferring them.

There are, of course, arguments for retaining such exchange fund system.[1] Briefly these are said to be: (1) it stabilizes exchanges and encourages trade, for if the balance of payments is adverse, gold needs not be exported, but payment will be made directly from the funds, thus keeping exchange up; and if the balance of payments is favorable,

[1] *Cf. e. g.*, T. Takayama, "Gold exchange fund system," *Ginko Kenkyu*, Dec., 1924, pp. 72-80.

gold is received abroad, thus reducing the ordinary gold import point still lower, giving favorable rates of exchange for Japanese exporters. But the argument against this system is the fact that such an operation belongs properly to the exchange bankers. Exchange banking to-day is far advanced over the time when such system was first adopted thirty-four years ago. Narrowing the spread of the specie points is possible only if the government had an unlimited amount of exchange funds abroad, or a continuous excess of receipts over payments,[1] which is not the case with Japan. (2) It is also said that the system can avoid inflation at home by keeping such funds as war indemnities and proceeds of foreign loans abroad. But the argument against this point is that nations without an exchange fund system do the same as Japan does. The modern method of the transfer of capital arises chiefly when exports do not pay imports, and is done mainly through bookkeeping on the part of international bankers. Therefore, Japan's keeping of financial agents abroad, such as agents of the Finance Department, agents of the Bank of Japan, besides giving or collecting financial reports, simply duplicates the work of bankers, which is quite wasteful. To the extent that these funds had been included for note-issuing purposes, it makes no great difference whether the funds were kept abroad or brought home. On the other hand, if they keep funds abroad, and the credits of such are not used at home, they are simply losing the difference of two interest rates; one being the interest that would have to be paid for the borrowed funds, ranging around 7 per cent, and the other being the interest that these funds can get while kept in a fluid form abroad, yielding not more than 3½ or 4 per cent. (3) Another argument for keeping the system is that it can stabilize the Japanese bonds abroad and can thereby maintain better

[1] Edgar S. Furniss, *Foreign Exchange*, New York, 1922, p. 129.

credit for Japan. But this is not so. This might have been the case thirty years ago. But to-day Japan's credit is not really dependent upon the amount of her gold holdings abroad, especially when they are accumulated by a series of foreign borrowings. To-day Japanese bonds are more dependent on Japan's earning capacity. And the earning capacity is judged more by her relative price movement, efficiency of labor and financial stability in general. To-day the old mercantilistic idea should be completely abandoned, while buying and selling of bonds should be entrusted to bankers and agents of bill-broking houses. (4) Lastly, the system is sometimes justified because expenditures of the Japanese government abroad, such as expenditures of diplomats, interest on foreign loans, etc., amount to more than 100 million yen every year. But such a claim as this fourth point is far from the avowed use of pegging exchange. Yet, granting that the system has this function also, it does not give enough weight or proof to the effect that the government agents can administer exchange banking better than the real exchange bankers.

Thus we come to believe that the exchange fund system has already outgrown its usefulness and is an entirely wrong system for Japan to pursue in to-day's international banking.

With the abolishment of the exchange fund system must come the free movement of gold, for free movement of gold insures the stability of exchanges and does away with the source of present speculation. But in order to bring about this change, it must avoid two things. One is a sudden exhaustion of gold reserve, inviting more exchange speculations; the other is a sudden fall of prices. The two are intimately connected with each other.

Certain economists like Dr. T. Fukuda of the Tokio College of Commerce and Dr. K. Horie of Keio University, and certain business men, like Mr. T. Muto of Kanezafuchi

Cotton Mill Company, and Dr. M. Takayanagi of the Osaka Chamber of Commerce, have been advocating ever since the great exchange slump of 1924 the immediate and complete lifting of the gold embargo. They believe that the lifting of the embargo and the immediate return to the gold standard would not only restore the exchanges immediately and keep them within the range of the specie points, but it would also hold gold within certain limits, for they contend that the export of gold would not continue for a long time, due to the fact that the lessening of gold lessens the currency in circulation, which in turn lowers prices, and lower prices in turn stimulate exports, and more exports not only promise to keep a favorable exchange rate, but also invite an inflow of gold, thus making a circulation of gold within a year or two. In other words, they applied the simple Ricardian theory of gold outflow and inflow. But the real situation in Japan is not so simple as that.

In the first place, a sudden lifting of the embargo would cause the prices of imported goods and other related goods to drop to the extent of the exchange slump. Take, for instance, 1924: imports were heavy with 2,451 million yen, in spite of the great exchange slump of from 20 to 24 per cent. Imports of subsequent years were likewise heavy, although exchange was steadily improving. Any sudden drop of prices, due to an artificial re-arrangement of specie-flow and, therefore, a general contraction of credits by the banks would certainly cause a panic. Therefore, the procedure of lifting the embargo must be slow and cautious when exchange is already at a great discount. Gold should not be exported all at once; but it must be limited to such an amount as would insure the stability of certain minimum rates of exchange. And in so far as the improvement of the purchasing-power parity takes place, and consequently in so far as the improvement of balance of payments takes place, gold exports may be increased to raise the exchange rate to the next higher stage where again within the minimum range of rates of that stage, gold may be more exported, and so on, step by step. But it is only when such raised rates reach near par backed by the better purchasing-power parity that the complete lifting of the gold embargo and finally the return to the gold standard may be recommended.[1]

Thus we have learned that debts and note issues should be limited in order to bring about a better purchasing-power parity for the yen. Better purchasing power parity will bring about better trade. Without the better balance of trade, the balance of payments cannot be improved for a country like Japan whose interests lie preponderantly in foreign commerce.[2]

As the yen is not employed like the dollar or the pound sterling by third countries in discharging their debts, yen exchange rates are largely determined in the long run by the above considerations. However, this does not mean that under the existing system of exchange pegging with gold funds abroad, speculation remains passive. On the contrary, speculation has influenced rates a great deal. The best way out is to abolish the system and lift the gold embargo when it becomes feasible to do so without any great friction either to business or to banking. The whole idea aimed at is not the gold standard but the stabilization of prices. Therefore, the means for returning to the gold standard, as well as to the object itself, should be to consider it from the point of view

[1] For such policy, I suggest the name "the step policy of raising foreign exchange."

[2] Mr. K. Kodama, governor of the Yokohama Specie Bank, calculated that nearly 60% of the total production in Japan is dependent on her export trade. (K. Kodama, "Japan's Future Finance, viewed from the Overseas Markets," *The Kokumin Shimbun*, Jan. 12, 1927.)

of stabilizing the yen internally first. Thus the stabilized yen, either on the way to the gold standard or already at the gold standard, will eliminate exchange fluctuations which are so demoralizing both to business and finance. And finally, the resumption of the gold standard without the exchange pegging system will limit enormously the possibilities of speculative manipulations and speculative raids. This will win for Japan the financial prestige in foreign money centers.

To sum up, in order to stabilize the Japanese exchange, three things are important. These are (1) to lower the general level of prices so that the purchasing power of the yen may be as high as that of the dollar or of the pound sterling, (2) to promote the visible and invisible trade so that the balance of international payments may turn favorable, and (3) to do away with the obvious and avoidable sources of exchange speculation. Such a practice as pegging by means of exchange funds is not only injurious to foreign trade but also very expensive. The so-called traditional policy of encouragement of exports and repression of imports was but one factor for exchange correctives. Moreover, even in order to bring about this commodity balance of trade, the relative price situation must be first considered; otherwise it is impossible to promote trade. In Japan a credit control under some *organized* banking system is highly desirable. If these big things are first accomplished, the small things, such as those advocated by the government, will be achieved, too, in due course.

CHAPTER VII

Conclusion: Test of Various Foreign Exchange Theories

I. THEORIES OF FOREIGN EXCHANGE

Today the Japanese are still following the Western theories. In matters of Foreign Exchange they have been more or less adhering to Goschen's theory as their intellectual guidance in various exchange fluctuations. For in Goschen [1] they have found the net results of classical theories which somehow satisfied the credulous minds of the Japanese before the War.

According to Goschen,[2] under ordinary circumstances where currency is stabilized, "interest of money, a balance of debts over claims, panic, distance, and so forth, practically cause the exchanges to vary within a few per cent; a variation of ten per cent owing to all these circumstances combined is considered something extraordinary and only occurs under rare combinations." For in most cases they are controlled by discount rates and their maximum fluctuations by the specie flow.[3] Of these elements, Goschen considers that (1) balance of indebtedness, and (2) interest rates are most important, and dwells much on them. According to him, an exporting country or a creditor country is likely to have "favorable" exchanges, because that country's money will

[1] Viscount G. G. Goschen, *Foreign Exchanges* (London, 1861), revised edition, 1863, and subsequent editions.

[2] G. G. Goschen, *ibid.*, pp. 64-65.

[3] G. J. Goschen, *ibid.*, pp. 43-57.

be dear or scarce in the exchange market; whereas a debtor country will suffer from adverse exchanges because that country's money will be offered redundantly in the market. But at the same time, high discount rates will attract money and check an outflow of specie.

But apart from these commonplace doctrines of exchange, Goschen introduces another factor, a more important factor for our purpose here, namely, "the depreciation of the currency." As soon as this factor is introduced, exchange may sink and rise much below the specie points. As an illustration of such instances, he cites slumps of 50 per cent in the Vienna and Russian exchanges during his day. He distinguishes, however, three principal types of such cases: (1) where bullion exports are not prohibited but are difficult; (2) where bullion exports are totally prohibited; and (3) where one country is a silver-standard and the other a gold-standard country.

Under the first situation the exchange will fluctuate "in proportion to the extent to which the prices of all purchasable articles—bullion included—are affected by the depreciation of the currency; in other words, in proportion to the discount of the paper money, or the premium on gold."[1] Beyond that proportion, it will not fluctuate, for if it did, despite the premium, it would be less expensive to ship gold than to buy bills at such an unfavorable rate. In the second case, where bullion exports are absolutely prohibited, Goschen finds that the limits on the fluctuations of the exchange are entirely removed. The price of bills of exchange is determined purely by their demand and supply alone.[2] In the third case, where trade is between a gold-standard and a silver-standard country, Goschen maintains that the par of exchange is established by the market ratio between the

[1] Goschen, *ibid.*, p. 69.

[2] Goschen, *ibid.*, pp. 70-72.

metals themselves. But since there will be a constant change in the ratio between these two metals along with a constant change in gold, as by supposition currency is depreciated, the limit of exchange fluctuations in this case is to the extent of the premium on gold.

These surprisingly clear and exact explanations of Goschen, however, were not altogether satisfactory to us, especially after 1916. For even under ordinary circumstances, where gold was freely moving, we found that the exchange was not always a dependent, passive, determined factor, but sometimes an independent, active, determining factor; just as in the theory of prices, price is not always determined by demand and supply, but it sometimes determines demand or supply. This was especially the case in the exchange speculation of 1924 and 1926. First the exchange went down; this influenced the prices of imported goods, as well as of exported goods.

The control of exchange by a discount policy is also absent from our experience. High interest rates did not always attract foreign capital. Although Goschen puts emphasis on the mechanical balancing of interest rates and the balance of foreign trade, he seems to have neglected the importance of such factors as the transfer of funds, the creation of credits, the payment of debts, and speculation. Actually, in the Japanese case, these have been more important factors than the interest rate. In fact, Goschen presupposes in his theory the existence of certain financial and banking mechanisms which Japan still lacks, and he assumes that everybody acts like an Englishman in the English market.

But more serious difficulties arise when it comes to his discussion of depreciated currencies. Goschen identifies, when paper is depreciated, the premium on gold with the level of prices. But in Japan such was not always the case. The premium on gold did not always coincide with the level of prices as measured by paper money. To illustrate, while the external value of the yen remained nearly constant, its internal value began to depreciate just a few months before the gold embargo was established. Conversely, while the internal value of the yen remained fairly constant in 1924, its external value depreciated beyond comparison.[1]

Moreover, under such circumstances, the gold flow was not the only adjuster of exchange rates. In Japanese exchange, at least, the transfer of funds has played a far more important rôle than the specie flow.

On the whole, Goschen confines himself to an analysis of the London exchange market of his day, and deduces the principle that the rates of exchange are determined by demand and supply of exchange bills. He has never gone far enough to analyze all those factors that influence the demand and supply of exchange bills. This defect of Goschen becomes more conspicuous when we try to apply his theory to the recent depreciated currency situation. Demand and supply must be explained in detail by the best of our modern business knowledge.

Such attempts have been made by such men as George Clare,[2] and Franklin Escher.[3] George Clare, for instance, brings out exhaustively in his book three main influences which directly affect the supply and demand of exchange bills; these are (1) trade influence, (2) stock exchange influence, and (3) banking influence. Under these three influences are included (1) imports and exports, (2) freights

[1] More familiar cases were England, France, Italy and Germany during 1919 to 1921. *See* Edgar S. Furniss, *Foreign Exchange*, Cambridge, 1922, p. 59.

[2] George Clare, *The A B C of the Foreign Exchange, a practical guide*, London, 1892, 5th edition, 1911.

[3] Franklin Escher, *The Elements of Foreign Exchange; a foreign exchange primer*, New York, 1910, 5th edition, 1916.

and the like, (3) securities, (4) interest on loans, (5) credits, (6) arbitrage, and (7) investments. But that was all. He never went beyond that. And so during the war and after the war when exchanges were greatly dislocated, the more serious thinkers could not understand what determined the exchange rate between two independent, depreciated countries. The Japanese were no exception. The ordinary European or American text-books on Foreign Exchange completely lacked an adequate answer to the problem. At this time Professor Gustav Cassel's purchasing-power-parity theory appeared, and was received at first with amusement [1] but later with admiration,[2] then followed by argument both for and against.

2. CASSEL'S THEORY OF THE PURCHASING POWER PARITY

In order to be just to Cassel and to understand the theory rightly, we must come to his celebrated book, *Money and Foreign Exchange after 1914*,[3] for in it we see his latest and presumably the final form of his presentation. All other sources must be subordinated to it.

Cassel's first and most important task as presented in this book is to understand the principal reason as to why foreign

[1] Gustav Cassel, "The Present Position of the Foreign Exchanges," *Economic Journal*, March, 1916, pp. 62-65; Sept., 1916, pp. 319-323; "Depreciation of Gold," *Economic Journal*, Sept., 1917; "Abnormal Deviations of International Exchanges," *Economic Journal*, Dec., 1918; "Depreciation of the Mark," *Economic Journal*, Dec., 1919. "Some Leading Propositions for an International Discussion of the World's Monetary Problem," *The Annals of the Am. Acad. of Pol. and Social Science*, May, 1920, pp. 259-267.

[2] His first memorandum for the Brussels International Monetary Conference, written June, 1920, and his second Memorandum for the Financial Committee of the League of Nations, written Oct., 1920, were received with much admiration for his insight and labor. Later these were published as *World's Monetary Problems: Two Memoranda*, London, 1921.

[3] Originally published in London, 1922.

exchanges, during the war, and especially after the war, were dislocated. In order to answer the question, he first analyzes the demand and supply of exchange bills. Of the demand he says, "our willingness to pay a certain price for foreign money must ultimately and essentially be due to the fact that this money possesses a purchasing power as against commodities and services in that foreign country."[1] That is, we demand foreign bills, principally because of their purchasing power. Likewise, of the supply, he says, "when we offer so-and-so much of our own money, we are actually offering a purchasing power as against commodities and services in our own country." That is, when we offer our bills, we are really offering our purchasing power. Therefore, he concludes that the exchange rate is "mainly dependent on the relative purchasing power of the two currencies in their respective countries."[2]

But this is only "a first and rough approximation." The fact that one had a foreign currency does not imply that one has, within one's own country, direct disposal over these commodities and services in that foreign country. One has to meet many difficulties such as divergencies in trade, transport, customs, etc. But apart from such *temporary* deviations, the relation of one inflated currency to the other remains intact and is best expressed by the relative purchasing powers. That is, suppose in country A the inflation went from 100 to 320, while in country B the inflation was only from 100 to 240. The relation of the two currencies is $\frac{240}{320}$ for A, or $\frac{320}{240}$ for B. In other words, the purchasing power of A's currency is now 75 over against B's 100, or A's currency lost its purchasing power by 25 per cent in respect

[1] Gustav Cassel, *Money and Foreign Exchange after 1914*, New York edition, 1925, p. 138.

[2] Cassel, *ibid.*, p. 139.

to B's currency. This relation of two currencies is called, according to Cassel, *the purchasing power parity*, because it is the parity of two purchasing powers. The parity or the rate thus calculated represents a new parity, and is regarded by Cassel as a *normal* or *real* ratio between two currencies around which, in spite of all temporary fluctuations, the actual exchange rates tend to move.[1]

This is Cassel's main proposition. The corollaries derivable from this proposition are, (1) the rate of exchange will not fall indefinitely, but will be equalized through international trade in accordance with the purchasing power parities, though abnormal, temporary deviations may occur, caused by (a) various restrictions in trade, (b) distrust in the future of the monetary standard or speculations, (c) the exports of capital or transfer of funds, (d) the failure of export prices to reflect the general price level closely, and (e) the deviation between the wage level and the general level of prices.[2] (2) Since the purchasing power parities are controllable mainly by the discount policy, the nations should exert their efforts toward this end, especially the United States, whose money is now the standard of all currencies.

Having stated the theory, let us now examine it. The most usual objection that we find in Japan is against its statistical basis. Perhaps the most typical of such objections is the one raised by Dr. Y. Takada of Kyushu Imperial University. In order to dispose the validity of the theory, he made a practical comparison between the Japanese-British parities and Japanese-French parities, and contrasted them with the actual exchange rates. Then he hastily complains that there was no close correlation in either of the two ex-

[1] Cassel, *ibid.*, pp. 139-140, also p. 156.

[2] Cassel, *ibid.*, pp. 147-158.

periments.[1] But his experiments were entirely inadequate to draw any definite conclusion. For he examined only a short period of hardly two and a half years, not by taking monthly averages, but by taking only a certain three months of the year which seemed best for his (Takata's) purposes. Such a comparison is itself statistically out of the question. But even in his case, the quotients of the two prices moved, speaking very roughly, in favor of correlation rather than of divergence.

Other critics doubted (a) the existence of the relation of the volume of note issue to the level of prices, and (b) that of general prices to the domestic prices. Regarding the first issue, this is clearly a case of misunderstanding. For Cassel explains the rise of prices not only by the expansion of notes, but also of private credits, where checks and bills are mostly used. "The primary cause is the artificial creation of the fresh purchasing power. This produces a rise in prices, and the rise in prices in turn renders necessary a proportional increase in the quantity of currency."[2] But for historical interest, as the Japanese are still using comparatively more notes than the Westerners, the writer has made a chart in which Japanese prices and the volume of bank notes are compared for the same period from 1914 to 1926, and found that there was a rather close correlation between the two, especially up to March, 1920, after which the two curves diverge more. On the whole, therefore, the above charge is groundless.

Regarding the second charge, critics argue that the prices

[1] Y. Takata, "Cassel's Theory of Foreign Exchange," The Keizai Ronso, VIII, No. 2; *A Study of Economics*, Tokio, 1924, pp. 725-737. The present writer was one of the first who introduced the theory into Japan. S. Y. Furuya, "Some criticisms on Cassel's theory of Foreign Exchange," *The Journal of Banking* (Ginko Kenkyu), Feb., 1923.

[2] Gustav Cassel, *Money and Foreign Exchange after 1914*, New York edition, 1925, p. 28.

of international commodities are different from those for purely home consumption. This charge is also strong in the United States where these prices diverge a great deal.[1] But with us the charge is rather imaginary than real. In the case of American foreign trade, the ratio of foreign trade to domestic trade, for instance, in 1919, was only about ten per cent,[2] whereas in Japan in that same year the ratio was 46 per cent.[3] Moreover, this comparatively more important foreign trade of Japan largely depends upon the export of raw silk and silk tissues, which in turn altogether made up in 1925, for instance, 43 per cent of the total exports. But the production of raw silk does not depend upon international element. Its cost of production is largely dependent on foodstuffs and wages. And wages in the country are in the long run largely expended domestic commodities. Therefore it is wrong to allege that this point is one of the fundamental defects of the theory. It would be far better for the critics to point out, for instance, some of the statistical defects in the structure of the Bank of Japan's index number. But as to the weight alone, it makes no vital difference whether it is weighted or unweighted, as already shown.[4]

[1] Wilhelm Keilhan, "The Valuation Theory of Exchange," *Economic Journal*, June, 1925, pp. 221-232; G. W. Terborgh, "The Purchasing Power Parity Theory," *Journal of Political Economy*, April, 1926, pp. 197-209.

[2] B. M. Anderson, in *The Income of the American People and the Ratio of Foreign Trade to Domestic Trade, 1890-1924*, The Chase National Bank, New York, Jan., 1925, p. 4 claims 19.5%.

[3] This figure was arrived at by the writer by the same method as employed by Anderson, basing, however, on the National Wealth of Japan as reported by the Government at the request of the League of Nations. *The Japan Year Book for 1926*, Tokio, p. 423. *See* also Mr. K. Kodama's figure, *supra*, p. 175.

[4] *See* page 111 and also Chart IV.

On the other hand, according to our survey as represented by Chart III, VIII and XI, in which monthly averages were taken for the determination of purchasing power parities over the period of thirteen years, 1914-1926, the following relationships were clearly shown: (1) When purchasing power parities moved favorably during the War,[1] the trend of yen exchange was also moving above par; but when the trend of parities went down in the next period,[2] the trend of exchange moved likewise below par, and when the parities began to improve after the beginning of 1925, the actual exchange also moved toward par.[3] This shows that, although there was no close correlation between the two *at a point of time,* yet *in the long run* there was a sort of correlation between the two movements. (2) The sequence of events was, first, the movement of the purchasing power parities of the yen; then the movement of the balance of payments, represented by the balance of trade; and lastly, the movement of the exchanges. From the point of view of a short-time analysis, however, certain exchange movements, such as the fall of 1924 and the rise of 1926, reacted on prices and trade considerably. (3) The above sequence of events was made possible, and the equilibrium of indebtedness was maintained, largely through (a) international trade, and, in a less degree, through (b) invisible trade, and (c) capital movements.

The two last statements need a little more explanation. The sequence of events was first characterized by a steady upward or favorable movement of purchasing power parities in the middle of 1914. Almost a year later this was followed by a favorable balance of trade. And nearly half a

[1] Chart III, p. 98; the period of 1914-1918.

[2] Chart VIII, p. 123; the period of 1919-1923.

[3] Chart XI, p. 149; the period of 1924-1926.

year later the exchanges crossed par and steadily went up.[1] The purchasing power parity reached its peak in March, 1917, while the excess of exports reached its peak in May, 1917 and the invisible balance of trade still lagged more, reaching its peak in 1918.[2] The capital movement also reached its peak, in favor of Japan, in 1918.[3] The exchange was last, reaching its peak in January, 1919.

The downward movements were also in the same order. The purchasing power parity started to decline steadily after March, 1917, crossing the 100 line in September, 1918, and reaching its bottom in October, 1921.[4] This was followed by the unfavorable balance of trade after the beginning of 1919, reaching a first low point in April, 1920 and the lowest point in March, 1924, while the invisible trade was gradually declining, reaching its minimum receipt in 1922,[5] and the capital movement reached its heaviest borrowing in 1924.[6] The exchange which began to decline after January, 1919, became unfavorable only after January, 1920. The biggest slump came in October, 1924, although this slump, as well as the recovery in 1926, was more due to exchange speculation.

Without such a general description of the long-run trend analysis, the purchasing-power-parity theory has no meaning in the history of Japanese exchange. But interpreted thus, it is perhaps the only explanation of how and why the Japanese exchange fluctuated to so high a point at one time and to so low a point at another time. That is to say, the theory is workable only in long-run terms, just as in the price

[1] *See* Chart III, p. 98.

[2] *See* the Table of Japan's invisible trade during the War, p. 62.

[3] *See* the Table of Capital movement during the War, p. 64.

[4] *See* Chart VIII, p. 123.

[5] *See* the Table of Invisible Trade after the War, p. 115.

[6] *See* the Table of Capital Movement after the Earthquake, p. 144.

theory, prices are determined in the long-run by the cost of production. But for short-time fluctuations, a somewhat different explanation must be sought. The purchasing-power-parity theory cannot withstand the shortcomings of index numbers, especially with respect to their base-year and the price-structure, as an indicator of temporary fluctuations of exchange. For exchange is perhaps the most sensitive price in the whole world, while an index number is but a rough approximation of the internal average value of a currency. How can two things of such different nature coincide?

3. KEYNES' REVISION

But before we pass to the opposite theories, J. M. Keynes' revision of Cassel's theory is noteworthy. His book, *A Tract on Monetary Reform* (London, 1923), came a year later and criticizes Cassel's theory at certain points. According to Keynes, (1) a "currency's internal purchasing power depends on the currency policy of the government and the currency habits of the people. . . . . (2) A currency's external purchasing power must be the rate of exchange between the home-currency and the foreign-currency, multiplied by the foreign-currency's purchasing power in its own country. (3) In conditions of equilibrium the internal and external purchasing powers of a currency must be the same, allowance being made for transport charges and import and export taxes. . . . (4) It follows, therefore, from (1), (2) and (3) that the rate of exchange between the home-currency and the foreign-currency must *tend* [1] in equilibrium to be the ratio between the purchasing powers of the home-currency at home and the foreign-currency in the foreign country. This ratio between the respective home purchasing powers of the two currencies is designated their purchasing power parity." [2] This is substantially the same that Cassel would

[1] The italics are mine.

[2] J. M. Keynes, *A Tract on Monetary Reform*, London, 1924, p. 88.

summarize today. But he goes on further to revise some of the minor points. The first is the choosing of the base-year, generally the year 1913, as the year in which the economic situation particularly in regard to transport and customs is to be taken as normal or standard, to which the comparison is made with other years. Naturally the purchasing power parity will be greatly affected according to what base year is taken.

Another difficulty according to Keynes is how to treat purchasing power over goods and services which do not enter into the international trade at all. Everybody knows that there is a divergence between indices of imported goods and exported goods. Moreover, labor and capital do not move freely between domestic and international industries. Yet in the purchasing-power-parity theory only the general level of prices is used. Therefore, Keynes concludes that if "we follow the ordinary practice of fixing purchasing power parity by comparison of the general purchasing power of a country's currency at home and abroad, then we must not infer from this that the actual rate of exchange ought to stand at the purchasing power parity, or that it is only a matter of time and adjustment before the two will return to equality. Purchasing power parity, thus defined, tells us an important fact about the relative changes in the purchasing power of money in (e. g.) England and the United States or Germany between 1913 and, say, 1923, but it does not necessarily settle what the equilibrium exchange rate in 1923 between sterling and dollars or marks ought to be."[1] Therefore, it is wrong, according to Keynes, to regard the purchasing power parity as if it were a rigid, accurate forecaster of actual exchanges; but it is a more trustworthy indicator in the long run.

Regarding these points, Cassel is not very clear except

[1] Keynes, *ibid.*, pp. 94-95.

that he makes an allowance for the temporary deviations. Nor does he differentiate between the short-run analysis and the long-run analysis. Keynes is, therefore, entitled to his revision. For the short-run analysis Keynes is of the opinion that reparation payments, financial deficits, seasonal trade balances, etc., are more responsible for exchange fluctuations.[1] But Keynes himself is not clear when he says, "in the long run" the purchasing power parity is "a more trustworthy indicator," how long a time has he in mind. Is it a week, month or year? Is it a seasonal trend, yearly trend or cyclical? He is utterly vague at this important point.

4. VARIOUS OPPOSITE THEORIES

Although Keynes revises Cassel's theory, yet his fundamental proposition belongs to Cassel. Somewhat the same attitude is taken by nearly all English economists. For instance, Professor Edwin Cannan says: "I am entirely in agreement with Professor Cassel's explanation of the general level of prices and of what is called the 'dislocation of exchanges.' . . . As to remedies, also I am in agreement with him. I am only inclined to add a little without taking away anything."[2] Professor A. C. Pigou, although it is true that he doubts the necessary relation between the domestic and international commodities, yet fundamentally agrees with Cassel and asserts that the "norm" of the exchange rates tends to move with, and to be governed by, the quotient between relative general price levels.[3] Others, like

[1] Keynes, *ibid.*, pp. 97, 107, 111, 112.

[2] Edwin Cannan, Comments on Professor Cassel's Article, in a symposium entitled "The World's Monetary Problems," *The Annals of the American Academy of Political and Social Science*, May, 1920, pp. 283-4.

[3] A. C. Pigou, "Some Problems of Foreign Exchange," *Econ. Jour.*, 1920, pp. 462-463. "The Foreign Exchanges," *Quarterly Journal of Economics*, Nov., 1922, pp. 62-67.

T. E. Gregory,[1] D. H. Robertson[2] and Hubert C. Walter[3] write in the same tone, with perhaps the single exception of A. W. Flux.[4]

In America, on the other hand, nearly all economists who have expresed their opinions regarding the theory are opposed to it, except Professor Irving Fisher,[5] who unreservedly supports the price-parity doctrine. Particularly noteworthy are those objections made by Dr. B. M. Anderson,[6] Professor James W. Angell,[7] and G. W. Terborgh.[8] On the whole, these objectors who make their arguments more or less from a theoretical standpoint point out the statistical defects of the quantity theory and defects in the formation of purchasing power parities, and put their stress on those very things Cassel took rather as an allowance for temporary deviations.

[1] T. E. Gregory, *Foreign Exchange, before, during and after the War*, London, 1922, pp. 87-93.

[2] D. H. Robertson, *Money*, New York, 1922, p. 137.

[3] Hubert C. Walter, *Foreign Exchange and Foreign Debts*, London, 1926, p. 153, *passim*.

[4] A. W. Flux, *Foreign Exchange*, London, 1924.

[5] Irving Fisher, in *The World's Monetary Problems* (cited above), p. 276. Among the business men, S. Stern is perhaps the strongest advocate of the price-parity theory, although he does not state it in terms of Cassel or Keynes. S. Stern, *The Foreign Exchange Problem, Columbia Trust Co.*, New York, 1921.

[6] B. M. Anderson, in *The World's Monetary Problems* (cited above), pp. 268-273, makes objections chiefly to the quantity theory on which the doctrine is based, assuming however, Cassel's quantity theory is similar to Fishers.

[7] J. W. Angell, in *The Theory of International Prices*, Cambridge, 1926, pp. 188-190, objects from two grounds: as a short-time analysis, the theory is not true; as a long-run analysis, the theory loses meaning since it does not seriously consider the more vital elements of fluctuations under the good name of allowance for temporary deviations.

[8] G. W. Terborgh, "The Purchasing Power Parity Theory," *The Journal of Political Economy*, April, 1926, pp. 197-209.

Quite different from the above are the objections based on some concrete observations made by the American economists. Professor Williams in his survey of German exchange and Professor Angell in his survey of British exchange both arrive at the opposite conclusion. According to J. H. Williams,[1] the German collapse of 1921 was neither due to the excessive issue of paper money nor to budget deficits, but due primarily to reparation payments. According to him, the sequence of events was, first, reparation payments; second, depreciation of exchange; third, general rise of prices headed by international commodities; fourth, consequential budgetary deficits and increased demand for bank credit; and lastly, increased note issue.[2] Likewise, J. W. Angell [3] asserts that "the English data cast a good deal of light on the purchasing-power-parity theory. They show that the order of exchange which that theory expects was on the whole reversed here, not confirmed. The exchanges moved first, then prices, and last of all the note circulation." He accounts for fluctuation of exchange by general speculation. But he does not say what are the causes for general speculation. Thus the American economists, on the whole, are quite opposed to the theory on the ground that for the short-run interpretation of the theory it is far from the concrete facts, and for the long-run analysis, to take away those elements of "temporary deviations" is virtually the same as to squeeze the theory into a meaningless and valueless entity. It is, however, a great irony to find that the U. S. Tariff Commission and the U. S. Senate Commission on

J. H. Williams, "German Foreign Trade and the Reparations Payments," *Quarterly Journal of Economics*, 1922, pp. 502-3.

[2] But the chief defect of Professor Williams's exposition, according to Professor Angell, was that he did not stress sufficiently the effects of speculation and anticipation. J. W. Angell, *ibid.*, p. 195.

[3] J. W. Angell, *ibid.*, p. 430.

Gold and Silver Inquiry, having investigated more or less the same data, seem to believe in the price-parity doctrine unreservedly. Their method of investigation closely follows the line of thought of Cassel's theory.[1]

While Professor Cassel's theory is thus being tested and re-tested in England and America, the Continental writers seem to be less interested in it. Dr. J. Van Walré de Bordes in *The Austrian Crown* seems to have written a standard work which makes a careful test of the price-parity theory. Dr. Bordes, who refers constantly to the latest works of Cassel and Keynes, after having examined the Austrian financial and exchange situation since 1914, arrives at a conclusion totally different from that inferable from Cassel. The collapse of the Austrian crown, both during and after the War, was wholly due to the lack of confidence on the part of foreigners as well as the people of Austria themselves. The lack of confidence, in turn, was due to " the rise of rates of exchange, the rise of prices, the increase of the velocity of circulation of money, the use of foreign notes as means of payment in Austria.[2] Thus the ordinary interpretation of Fisher's equation of exchange [3] is contradictory to his findings. According to him, in Austria, "during a period of heavy depreciation, the prices were influenced chiefly by an outside factor, the foreign exchange rates, and were therefore no longer a mere passive element in the

[1] U. S. Tariff Commission, *Depreciated Exchange and International Trade*, Washington, 1922, pp. i, ii, 12, 16. U. S. Senate Commission on Gold and Silver Inquiry. *Foreign Currency and Exchange Investigation*, Series 9, Washington, 1925, vol. i, pp. xv, 35, 37-39, *passim*; vol. ii, pp. 22-23, 48, 69, 93, 118, 156, *et seq.*, *passim*.

[2] J. van Walre de Bordes, *The Austrian Crown, London*, 1924, p. 197.

[3] He modifies Fisher's formula $M \times V' + M' \times V'$ to $P \times G \times S$; G being the average quantity of goods in circulation and S being the average velocity of circulation of goods. He asserts that the casual relations between the two sides of the equation are mutual and independent. de Bordes, *ibid.*, pp. 154-178.

equation of exchange. Thus during the period of severe depreciation we see in Austria, first a rise in the rates of exchange, secondly a rise of prices, and only as a final development an increase of the note circulation, the very converse in fact of what might have been expected according to the ordinary quantity theory and the purchasing-power-parity theory." [1] Accordingly he suggests an amendment to the purchasing-power-parity theory by saying that the theory should state that "during periods of depreciation, the rates of exchange tend to coincide, not with the actual, but the *expected future purchasing power parity*." [2] In other words, the foreign exchange market, according to him, may be so completely dominated by speculation and movements of capital that the rates of exchange may move independently of the purchasing power parity, i. e. of the price levels.

But like most objectors to the parity theory, he does not go a step further and analyze what are some of the elements that make for speculation and movements of capital. Nor does he make a distinction between the short-run trend and the long-run trend of the exchange movements, a distinction which is very important in any price analysis.

Outside of de Bordes, those in Europe who have made a careful study of the recent foreign exchange problems worthy of mention here along with other authorities (not to mention various doctor's dissertations which are more or less of classical thought) are Professors Charles Rist [3] and Bertrand Nogaro [4] in France and Dr. Karl Diehl [5] in Germany.

[1] de Bordes, *ibid.*, p. 198.

[2] de Bordes, *ibid.*, pp. 198-199.

[3] C. Rist, *La deflation en pratique*, Paris, 1924.

[4] B. Nogaro, *La monnaie et les phenomenes contemporains*, Paris, 1924.

[5] Karl Diehl, *Uber Fragen des Geldwesens und der Valuta wahrend des Krieges und nach dem Kriege*, Zweite Aufl., Jena, 1921.

Professor C. Rist, after having made a survey of the English, American, French and Czecho-Slovakian exchanges from 1919 to 1923, concludes that the causes of present abnormal dislocation of exchanges are found in the financial dislocation of the countries involved. Prices and exchanges are both the result of certain budgetary disorganization. According to him, the increase of money due to budgetary needs is the cause of high prices and of dislocated exchanges; but when exchanges are already dislocated and prices are already high, exchanges may become a cause of further increase of money.[1] But since the general cause of depreciation lies in the budgetary situation, the recovery of exchanges may be attained only through the equilibrium of the budget. But Professor Nogaro holds a somewhat different position. According to him, the exchange depreciation was largely due to speculation. And he considers that exchange depreciation first took place. This was then followed by the change in the price-situation. To re-enforce these statements Nogaro illustrates the post-war conditions of France, Germany, England, Czecho-Slovakia and Austria.

Thus Rist and Nogaro are opposed to the purchasing-power-parity theory. But when they come to their own theory, they differ from each other. In reading them, one cannot but feel that at least one account of causation, particularly from exchanges to prices, is most dubious, for contradictory opinions regarding the same facts cannot be both right.

In Germany most writers are anti-quantity theorists. In regard to the recent exchange problems, Dr. Karl Diehl's position may be taken as representative of the German opinion. According to him, the chief cause of the depreciation of the German exchanges has not been the depreciation of currency itself, but the adverse balance of trade and pay-

[1] C. Rist, *ibid.*, pp. 113-130.

ments. In other words, according to him, the primary cause is the balance of payments; the secondary cause is the depreciation of currency. The other causes, such as speculation and political influences, are the result of and attached to the primary cause.[1] He reaches this conclusion by, first, examining the German foreign trade with the neutral countries in the beginning of the War; and, second, by ascertaining the one-sided payment; and, lastly, by alleging speculation and political events.[2] Thus he opposes Cassel's early formulation of an "inflation" theory,[3] and rather takes the scarcity of commodities as the chief cause of high prices and hence the unfavorable balance of payments.[4] But as he does not present any extensive statistical verification to prove his case, and as we are presented with contradictory interpretations by other authorities, we are puzzled whether we should follow his line of thought or Cassel's, or even Nogaro and de Bordes's line of thought. None of these is quite convincing.

On the other hand, the survey of the Japanese yen above clearly reveals that the factors connected with exchange fluctuations are *many* and of two classes, one being of a temporary and the other of a more permanent character. One is governed by speculation, selling and buying of exchange funds, and transfer of funds, while the other is guided by the purchasing power parity. In the former case, exchange often reacts on prices. But this is only for a short-time interval. In the latter case or in the long run, if the trend of purchasing power parities long favors Japan, the exchange is largely governed by the relative prices

[1] Karl Diehl, *ibid.*, S. 38.

[2] Karl Diehl, *ibid.*, SS. 39-52.

[3] Gustav Cassel, *Deutchlands wirtschaftliche Widerstandskraft*, Berlin, 1916, S. 133, *cf.* K. Diehl, *ibid.*, S. 53, *passim*, SS. 66-86.

[4] Karl Diehl, *ibid.*, S. 67.

through the balance of international payments. Such a distinction seems to be imperative in explaining the Japanese yen fluctuations, although in reality the two classes of factors are interdependent.

5. CONCLUSION

To recapitulate the results obtained: we have seen that there are at least six theories of Foreign Exchange that are still advocated today. These are that the recent dislocation is due to:

(1) The balance of trade (usually takes the form of excess of imports over exports).
(2) The balance of payments (usually takes the simple form of demand and supply).
(3) The purchasing power parity (this again differs between Cassel's form and Keynes' form).
(4) Speculation.
(5) The balance of payments and speculation (this again differs according to each writer, but is chiefly advocated by the American economists, especially by men like A. A. Young, J. H. Williams and J. W. Angell).
(6) Above, (3) and (5) (this is to be advocated by the writer in this conclusion).

These theories differ from each other in respect to (a) factors in exchange fluctuations, (b) the sequence of events, and (c) the time involved. Let me re-state each briefly, and then establish the theoretical basis of my conclusion.

(1) Balance of trade (or excess of imports over exports). T. E. Gregory thinks that "exchange experts at the present time divide themselves into two camps: those who think that the exchanges are dislocated because of inflation, and those who think that they are dislocated because

of 'an excess of imports over exports'."[1] But those who think that the exchanges are dislocated because of adverse trade are comparatively few today among the economists, although among business men and bankers there are still found many of this type. This simple form of classical tenet is more true of the backward and small country whose relatively small international indebtedness consists chiefly of commodity trade and of few transfers of funds. Applied to the modern progressive states, the balance of trade is only one item of the balance of payments; it alone cannot determine the exchange. Moreover, it is doubtful whether the adverse trade balance is a cause or an effect of exchanges. One cannot always explain the exchange fluctuations in terms of balance of trade.

(2) Balance of payments (or a simple form of supply and demand). Many text-books on Foreign Exchange have been written even since 1914. But only a few aim to give answers to the modern exchange phenomena. Most text-books give a scant explanation of the demand-and-supply theory. That exchange is determined by demand and supply of bills of exchange in the market is of course true, and will hold for actual cases as far as their statement goes. But my complaint is that they do not go far enough. What are the forces working behind demand? And what are the forces acting behind supply? How do they work in the short run? In the long run? Are the exchanges always determined or are they determining? What relation have they to the general level of prices or to the internal value of money? The text-books, without giving some explanation to these questions are certainly antiquated, at least, for the use of up-to-date students of international banking.

(3) The purchasing power parity. The theory of the

[1] T. E. Gregory, *Foreign Exchange before, during and after the War*, Oxford, 1922, Preface, p. 7.

purchasing power parity as it is left by Cassel is too vague for any practical application. Keynes' revision is, therefore, noteworthy. The price-parity doctrine as a short-run explanation is misleading. The calculated parities do not coincide with, nor move closely with actual exchanges. As a long-run explanation it is meaningful. It does explain the general tendencies of exchange movements. But Keynes is not clear as to how long a time is involved in such long-run analysis. On the whole, he seems to be too optimistic with the practical application of the theory. On the other hand, to reject the theory entirely is to ignore a great contribution that Cassel so opportunely made.

(4) Speculation. Certain economists and government officials are always eager to emphasize the element of speculation more than its due amount. Indeed, speculation has been made the scapegoat for the rise in foreign exchanges or for the fall in the international value of the home currency, in much the same way that speculators in commodities have been accused of causing a general rise in commodity prices within a country. Speculation may be predominantly and often is the cause of fluctuations for a short time, especially when political, economic and fiscal conditions are not settled. But it is evident that it cannot be the sole cause of exchange fluctuations for all time and all places. The causation is not always from exchanges to prices, but it may be the other way. On the whole, the monistic view of causation in the field of economic law is most dangerous, as by nature economic law is the combination of historical law and natural experimental law.[1]

(5) Balance of payments and speculation. This is the most ordinary form of the theories of the objectors to the price-parity doctrine. Professor J. W. Angell and Dr. de

[1] K. Soda, *Die logische Natur der Wirtschaftsgesetze*, Tübinger staatswissenschaftliche Abhandlungen, 17, Stuttgart, 1911, S. 96.

Bordes are perhaps the outstanding exponents of this theory. Equipped with all the factors that enter the balance of payments and speculation, they claim that demand and supply of exchange bills are well explained, and that the causation is from exchanges to prices, although they admit that in some cases the sequence of events may be the other way. But is this the final refinement? Apparently not. The theory seems to be equipped with all elements for the short-time fluctuations of exchange, but it lacks the explanation of that big predominating force working under all of those elements, namely, the trend of price parities. The lack of explanation of price parities in accounting for the dislocation of exchanges is like ignoring the increase of the means of payments in accounting for the rise of prices. In other words, to omit the element of purchasing power parity in the long-run analysis of recent dislocated exchanges is to ignore a great contribution made by Cassel and Keynes in the field of foreign exchange after the War.

Furthermore, this type of theory does not make a short-time and long-time analysis, a method long before employed in price determination by J. S. Mill and more successfully in the form of normal and market price by Alfred Marshall.[1] The complicated modern price phenomena need some such device in order to differentiate the causes of temporary fluctuations from those of more permanent character.

(6) My own theory. My own theory of exchange is the combination of the above (3) and (5). This form of theory will meet the defects of the purchasing-power-parity theory by supplementing it with the theory of temporary fluctuations. As to the elements, it embraces all. It reckons both short-time and long-time analysis. As to causation, the movement of actual exchange rates in the long-run tends to follow the trend of the purchasing power parity. That is, the trend of

[1] Alfred Marshall, *Principles of Economics*, 3rd ed., pp. 441-2.

price parities determines the general *long-run* position of actual exchanges. On the other hand, just exactly where that position will be is determined by such factors as balance of trade, invisible trade, transfer of funds and speculation. These are the *short-run* determinants. In the latter case the exchange movement will be a cause of the change of prices, whereas in the former case the exchange movement may be a result of the change of prices. The two, however, do not act entirely separately and independently. The two are interwoven. One acts on the other and is reacted upon by the other. But on the whole, the temporary fluctuations themselves come under the general influence of the trend of purchasing power parities. The result of our survey of Japanese exchange fluctuations clearly verifies these statements. To repeat, we may tabulate as follows.

(1) Long-time explanation:

First, we have seen that, when the trend of purchasing power parities were moving low during the period of 1900-1914, the movement of the yen exchange was also below the par line; but when the trend of the parity went up during 1914-1918, the exchange was also moving up; but when the parity was recovering after 1924, the yen was also recovering. The lead of purchasing power parity and the lagging of exchange in the long-run analysis have been statistically proved and shown by Charts III, VIII and XI.

Secondly, we have noticed that in our case the sequence of events was, first, changes in the purchasing power parity, then changes in the balance of payments, especially the balance of commodity trade, and lastly, changes in the exchange rates. This is why we have found that if the balance of trade was favorable for some time, say at least three to four years, the exchange was also favorable. But the purchasing power parity has never been directly reflected in the exchange. It ought to go through the balance of visible and invisible trades and transfer of funds—in short, through the balance of internatonal payments. The time involved was, therefore, necessarily long.

(2) Short-time explanation:

Thirdly, we have observed that for short-time or temporary exchange fluctuation speculation was often responsible. Thus we have found that the Shanghai exchange in 1916 and 1917, the New York exchange in 1920, the great slump of the yen in 1924, the recovery in 1926, and a temporary dip in April, 1927 were all due to exchange speculation. Of course, other factors were there; but they did not lead the movement. The causes which worked behind speculation were numerous, such as political changes, economic and social disturbance and natural calamity. Backed by speculation, the actual supply and demand of exchange bills in the market are of course the determining factors.

(3) Relation between short-time and long-time factors and exchange rates:

Fourthly, we have seen that all of these factors are working together behind the supply and demand of yen exchange bills. None of them could act quite independently of others. The short-time factors act more like ripples in the ocean while the long-time factors behave more like big waves. But when such things as the great earthquake, an enormous excess of imports, bank failures, etc., occurred, speculation always came to the forefront and influenced the demand and supply of the yen more than anything else. Under normal conditions, therefore, the purchasing power parity (long-time factor), speculation (short-time factor) and the balance of payments (both long-time and short-time factors) are the three most important factors which influence the exchange rates. But at the same time, the exchange rates themselves are constantly influencing one or all of these factors. Both, the factors of exchange and the exchanges themselves, are interdependent.

Thus the theory of foreign exchange I have arrived at deductively here coincides with the conclusion I have inductively reached by the survey of the Japanese exchange. The correctives for the yen exchange which I have proposed at the end of the last chapter are, therefore, also shown to be sound, in the light of this theoretical analysis. Furthermore, the theory of foreign exchange here expounded is not separate and distinct from my general theory of prices: it is only one application or one form of that general theory of prices.[1] This theory of foreign exchange is, therefore, free from internal contradiction.

[1] *Vide*, S. Y. Furuya, Keizai genron (Principles of Economics), Kyoto, 1925, chapters on prices.

APPENDIX A

Bibliography

In the following bibliography, only those books, monographs, pamphlets, journals and newspapers that are directly consulted in this work are given. Books which may serve as references are consciously omitted.

JAPANESE GOVERNMENT PUBLICATION

Bureau de la statistique générale, *Resumé statistique de l'empire du Japan*, Tokio, 1925.

Department of Commerce and Industry, *Kaigai Boeki Gairyaku (Summary of Foreign Trade of 1926)*, Tokio, 1927.

Department of Finance, *Kinyu Jikō Sankosho (Matters relating to Finance)*, vols. for 1924, 1925, 1926, Tokio, 1924-1926.

——, *The Twenty-fifth (and Twenty-sixth) Financial and Economic Annual of Japan*, vols. of 1926 and 1927, Tokio, 1926-1927.

——, *The National Debts of Japan*, Tokio, 1906.

——, *Financial Statistics of Japan*, Tokio, 1923.

——, *The Quarterly Report of Finance and Economic Conditions of Japan* (quarterly), nos. 3, 4, 5, Tokio, 1925-1926.

——, *Annual Return of the Foreign Trade of the Empire of Japan*, Tokio, 1926.

——, *Monthly Return of the Foreign Trade of the Empire of Japan*, vols. December, 1926, January, 1927, Tokio, 1927.

Department of Interior, *The Forty-fifth Statistics of the Japanese Empire*, Tokio, 1926.

Allen, G. C., "Recent Currency and Exchange Policy of Japan," *Econ. Jour.*, Mar., 1925.

Anderson, B. M., *The Income of the American People and the Ratio of Foreign Trade to Domestic Trade*, 1890-1924, The Chase National Bank, N. Y., 1925.

Angell, James W., *The Theory of International Prices*, Cambridge, 1926.

——, "International Trade under Inconvertible Paper," *Quar. J. of Econ.*, 1922, vol. 36.

——, "Monetary Theory and Monetary Policy," *Quar. J. of Econ.*, Feb., 1925.

The Asahi Shimbun, *English Supplement, Present Day Japan*, Osaka, June, 1927.

Bank of Japan, *Economic Statistics of Japan*, Tokio, 1925.

——, *Oshu Senso to Nippon Kinyukai* (*The European War and the Japanese Financial Market*), Tokio, 1918.

Bureau of Foreign and Domestic Commerce (U. S. A.), *China, a commercial and industrial handbook*, Washington, 1926.

——, *Trend in Japanese Trade*, Washington, 1926 (by H. A. Butts), Washington, 1926.

de Bordes, J. van Walre, *The Austrian Crown*, London, 1924.

Buchanan, Daniel H., "The Rural Economy of Japan," *Q. J. of Econ.*, Aug., 1923, pp. 545-578.

Cannan, Edwin, Comments on Professor Cassel's article: "The World's Monetary Problems," *The Annals of the American Academy of Pol. and Social Science*, May, 1920.

Cassel, Gustav, *Money and Foreign Exchange after 1914* (London, 1922), New York edition, 1925.

——, *World's Monetary Problems, Two Memoranda*, London, 1921.

——, "Present Position of the Foreign Exchange," *Econ. Jour.*, March and September, 1916.

——, "Depreciation of Gold," *Econ. Jour.*, September, 1917.

——, "Abnormal Deviations of International Exchanges," *Econ. Jour.*, December, 1918.

——, "Depreciation of the Mark," *Econ. Jour.*, December, 1919.

——, "Some Leading Propositions for an International Discussion of the World's Monetary Problem," *The Annals of the American Academy of Political and Social Science*, May, 1920.

——, *Deutchlands wirtschaftliche Widerstandskraft*, Berlin, 1916.

——, *Theoretische Sozialokonomie*, Dritte, verbesserte Aufl., Leipzig, 1923.

Chablani, H. S., *Indian Currency and Exchange*, Madras, 1925.

Clare, George, *The A B C of the Foreign Exchange* (London, 1892), revised ed., 1911.

Cross, Ira B., *Domestic and Foreign Exchange*, New York, 1923.

Diehl, Karl, *Uber Fragen des Geldwesens und der Valuta wahrend des Krieges und nach dem Kriege*, Zweite Aufl., Jena, 1921.

Eddins, George E., "International Silver Market," *Commerce Monthly*, October, 1926.

Edwards, George W., *Investing in Foreign Securities*, New York, 1926.

Escher, Franklin, *The Elements of Foreign Exchange, a Foreign Exchange Primer*, New York, 1910.

Federal Reserve Board, *Prices in the United States and Abroad*, 1919-1923, Washington, 1923.

——, Federal Reserve *Bulletin* (monthly), vols. 1915-1927, Washington, 1915-1927.

Fisher, Irving, Comments on Cassel's "The World's Monetary Problems," *The Annals of the Am. Acad. of Pol. and Soc. Sc.*, May, 1920.

Flux, A. W., *Foreign Exchange*, London, 1924.

Furniss, Edgar S., *Foreign Exchange, the Financial Mechanism of International Commerce*, Boston, 1922.

Furuya, S. Y., *Foreign Exchange*, Kyoto, revised ed., 1925.

——, *Keizai Genron*, Kyoto and Tokio, 1925.

——, "Japan's Foreign Exchange Policy," *Doshisha Law Review*, November, 1924.

——, "The Keynote of Japan's Exchange Policy," special edition of the *Fujimoto Weekly*, January, 1925.

——, "Recent Theories of Foreign Exchange," *The Ginko Kenkyu* (Banking Monthly), December, 1924.

Gide, Charles, "French War Budgets for 1919-1920," *Econ. Jour.*, June, 1919.

Goschen, G. G., *Foreign Exchanges* (London, 1861), revised edition 1863.

Gregory, T. E., *Foreign Exchange, before during and after the War*, London, 1922.

——, *The Return to Gold*, London, 1925.

Herzfelder, Edmund, *Die volkswirtschaftliche Bilanz und eine neue Theorie der Wechselkurse*, Berlin, 1919.

Inoue, Junnosuke, *Sengoni okeru Wagakunino Kinyu oyobi Keizai (Japan's Financial and Economic Conditions after the War)*, Tokio, 1925.

——, *Wagakunino Kokusai Kinyu no Genjo oyobi sono Kaizensaku (Japan's International Finance at Present and her Policy)*, Tokio, 1926.

—— "Present Financial Condition," *Jitsugyono Nippon*, Tokio, July, 1927.

Jaeger, Ruth M., *Stabilizing of the Foreign Exchanges*, Columbia, 1924.

The Japan Times, "Economic Development of Korea and Manchuria," Tokio, 1923.

The Japan Year Book, 2 vols., 1926 and 1927, Tokio, 1926-1927 (editor, Takenonu).

Kashiwagi, H., "The Japanese Yen and Japan's Economic Condition," *The Foreign Securities Investor*, March, 1926.

Keilhan, Wilhelm, "The Valuation Theory of Exchange," *Econ. Jour.*, June, 1925.

Kellenberger, Eduard, *Wechselkurs and Zahlungsbilanz im Kriege und Frieden*, Zürich, 1919.

Keynes, J. M., *A Tract on Monetary Reform*, London, 1924.

Kodama, Kenji, "Japan's Future Finance viewed from the Overseas Markets," *The Kokumin Shimbun*, No. 12,567.

Kobayashi, U., *War and Armament Loans of Japan*, New York, 1922.
Kurisu, O., *Nippon Kinyushi no Kenkyu* (*A Study on History of Finance in Japan*), Tokio, 1927.
Kyoto Imperial University, *Kyoto University of Economic Review*, No. 1, July, 1926.
League of Nations, *Memorandum on Currency and Central Banks*, 1913-1925, Geneva, 1926.
——, *Memorandum on Balance of Payments and Foreign Trade*, Geneva, 1925.
——, *Brussels Financial Conference*, Geneva, 1923.
Leurence, Fernand, *La stabilisation du Franc*, Paris, 1926.
Maeda, K., *Yen Gawaseno Kenkyu* (*A Study of Japanese Yen Exchange*), Tokio, 1925.
Mahlberg, Walter, *Uber asiatische Wechselkurse*, Leipzig, 1920.
Matsukata, M., *Report on the Adoption of the Gold Standard in Japan*, Tokio, 1899.
Mitchell, Wesley C., *International Price Comparisons*, Washington, 1919.
The New York Journal of Commerce, "A History of Banking in All Leading Nations," New York, 1896.
Nogaro, B., *La monnaie et les phenomene contemporaine*, Paris, 1924.
Odate, G., *Japan's Financial Relations with the United States*, Columbia, 1922.
The Oriental Economist Year Book, Tokio, 1925.
Pigou, A. C., "Some Problems of Foreign Exchange," *Econ. Jour.*, January, 1920.
——, "The Foreign Exchange," *Quar. J. of Econ.*, November, 1922.
Prion, W., *Inflation und Geldentwertung*, Berlin, 1919.
Remer, C. F., *The Foreign Trade of China*, Shanghai, 1926.
Rist, Charles, *La deflation en pratique*, Paris, 1924.
Robertson, D. H., *Money*, New York, 1922.
Saito, Hiroshi, "The Natural Resources of Japan," *The Ann. of Am. Acad. of Pol. and Soc. Sci.*, vol. 122, November, 1925.
Schacht, H., *Die Stabilisierung der Mark*, Berlin, 1927.
Seligman, Edwin R. A., *Principles of Economics*, 11th ed., New York, 1926.
The Silk Association of America, *The Fifty-fifth Annual Report*, New York, 1927.
——, *The Twenty-seventh Mid-Year Report*, New York, 1926.
Soda, Kiichiro, *Die logische Natur der Wirtschaftsgesetze*, Stuttgart, 1911.
Soyeda, J., "Economic Situations in Japan," *Econ. Jour.*, June, 1923.
Spalding, W. F., *Eastern Exchange, Currency and Finance* (London, 1917), fourth ed., London, 1924.

The Statesman's Year Book, vols. 1918-1926, London, 1918-1926.

Statistical Abstract for British India from 1915-16 to 1924-25, London, 1926.

Stern, S., *The Foreign Exchange Problem*, The Columbia Trust Co., New York, 1921.

Takata, Y., *Keizaigaku Kenkyu*, Tokio, 1924.

Takayama, T., "The Gold Exchange Fund System," *Ginko Kenkyu*, December, 1924.

Taussig, F. W., *International Trade*, New York, 1927.

Terborgh, G. W., "The Purchasing Power Parity Theory," *J. of Pol. Econ.*, April, 1926.

Uyehara, U., *The Industry and Trade of Japan*, London, 1926.

U. S. Senate, Commission of Gold and Silver Inquiry, *Foreign Currency and Exchange Investigation*, vols. i-ii, Washington, 1925 (editor, John Parke Young).

——, Depreciated Exchange and International Trade, Washington, 1922.

van Dorp, E. C., "Abnormal Deviations in International Exchanges," *Econ. Jour.*, 1920.

——, "Deviations of Exchange," *Econ. Jour.*, vol. 29, 1919.

Walter, Hubert C., *Foreign Exchange and Foreign Debts*, London, 1926.

Whitaker, A. C., *Foreign Exchange*, New York, 1919.

Wikawa, T., "Sources of Revenue in Japan," *The Ann. of Am. Acad. of Pol. and Soc. Sc.*, November, 1925.

Williams, J. H., "German Foreign Trade and the Reparation Payments," *Quar. J. of Econ.*, 1922.

——, "Prices and the Course of International Trade," *The Ann. of Am. Acad. of Pol. and Soc. Sc.*, May, 1920.

——, "Foreign Exchanges under Depreciated Paper," *Jour. of Am. Bankers Association*, 1922.

Willis, H. Parker and Edwards, *Banking and Business*, New York, 1925.

Willis, H. Parker and Steiner, William H., *Federal Reserve Banking Practice*, New York, 1926.

Willis, H. Parker, *History of the Federal Reserve System*, New York, 1924.

Withers, Hartley, *Money Changing*, London, 1913.

The World's Almanac (for 1926 and 1927), New York, 1926-1927.

Yamamuro, S., *Waga kunino Kinyu Shijo* (*Financial Market in Japan*), Tokio, 1926.

York, Thomas, *International Exchange, Theory and Practice*, New York, 1923.

Young, A. A., "War Debts, External and Internal," *Foreign Affairs*, 1924.

Yhuka, T., "Why no Discount Market in Japan," *The Kokumin Shimbun*, January 20-22, 1927.

Zimand, Savel, *State Capitalism in Russia*, New York, 1927.

Bei Fragen zur Produktsicherheit wenden Sie sich bitte an:
If you have any questions regarding product safety,
please contact:

Walter de Gruyter GmbH
Genthiner Straße 13
10785 Berlin
productsafety@degruyterbrill.com